A Big Splash in a Small Pond

Finding a Great Job in a Small Company

R. Linda Resnick
with Kerry H. Pechter

WITHDRAWN

A Fireside Book
Published by Simon & Schuster

New York   London   Toronto   Sydney   Tokyo   Singapore

FIRESIDE
Rockefeller Center
1230 Avenue of the Americas
New York, New York 10020

FIRESIDE and colophon are registered trademarks
of Simon & Schuster Inc.

DESIGNED BY BARBARA MARKS
Manufactured in the United States of America

1   3   5   7   9   10   8   6   4   2

Library of Congress Cataloging-in-Publication Data
is available.

ISBN: 0-671-79807-3

Contents

Acknowledgments   9

Foreword
**William C. Dunkelberg, Dean of the School of Business
and Management, Temple University**   *15*

Preface
Manage Your Job Search Like a Small Business   *19*

Introduction
Why Look for a Job in a Small Company?   *25*

PART ONE
UNDERSTANDING THE SMALL-BUSINESS JOB MARKET   *31*

Chapter One
**Small Businesses, Like Fish, Come in All Shapes
and Sizes**   *35*

Chapter Two
**Comparing Small-Company Ponds to
Large Corporate Oceans**   *55*

Chapter Three
**The Bullfrog: Understanding the Mind
of the Small-Company CEO**   *65*

Chapter Four
The Female of the Species: The Lady Bullfrog *80*

Chapter Five
**Dissecting the Bullfrog: How to Understand
the Various Types of Small-Business Employers** *92*

Chapter Six
What Small-Company Managers Really Do *99*

**PART TWO
FINDING A JOB IN THE SMALL-BUSINESS MARKET** *109*

Chapter Seven
**Getting to Know Your Skills, Abilities,
and Preferences** *113*

Chapter Eight
**Ten Personality Traits That Predict Success
in Small Business** *125*

Chapter Nine
Weaving Your Small-Business Network *132*

Chapter Ten
Gathering Information About Small Companies *149*

Chapter Eleven
**Customizing Your Small-Business Resume
and Cover Letter** *161*

Chapter Twelve
**Facing the Bullfrog: The Small-Company
Job Interview** *177*

Chapter Thirteen

Digging Your Own Pond: How Four Big-Company Professionals Started Businesses of Their Own *195*

Epilogue

Manage Your Job Search Like a Small Business, Revisited *207*

Bibliography *211*

Index *215*

Acknowledgments

This book is a product of the networking methods that it espouses. In fact I can't think of a better illustration of the power of networking than the story of how this book came to be.

More than 100 business people in my professional and personal networks, and in my coauthor's network, provided the information and advice we needed to research, write, and edit this book. Many of them, in turn, introduced us to people in their networks. Networking *works*, and this book proves it.

It all started when I placed an ad in the *National Business Employment Weekly* in early 1991 to publicize my seminar, "How to Get a Job in a Small Company."

Although my seminar was limited at that time to the Philadelphia area, the inquiries I received from thousands of miles away told me that a large national audience might exist for a book about the small-business job market.

Never having written a book, I turned to my network for help. My friend Chrissa Merron sent me to her friend, Peggy Anderson, author of *Nurses*, who generously recommended me to her literary agent, Jane Dystel of Acton & Dystel, Inc., in New York.

When I needed the assistance of a professional writer, I consulted Barrie Atkin, a friend and management consultant with ties to the publishing industry. She led me to my coauthor, Kerry Pechter, with whom she'd edited a newsletter at Rodale Press.

Through each step of the process the network responded to our needs. While preparing the book proposal and drafting a contract, we received valuable assistance from the writer Deborah Spungen, author of *And I Don't Want to Live This Life Anymore*, to whom my friend Nancy Osman referred me. Gerald Elman, an intellectual property attorney whom I knew through my synagogue, advised us on the details of the contract.

When Jane Dystel circulated our proposal among her network of book editors, we were fortunate to meet Edward Walters of Simon & Schuster, who became our editor. Ed was receptive to our ideas, offered us insights into the world of publishing, and provided key recommendations throughout the process.

To find people who could help me research the book, I turned to those I'd met through my professional networks. My contacts in the Pennsylvania Innovation Network, the Temple University School of Business and Management's Entrepreneurial Institute, the Forum of Executive Women of Delaware, the Omega Institute's Workshop on Socially Responsible Business, and the Philadelphia Human Resource Planning Group all provided valuable information.

Some of the executives in those networks later attended our focus group on the hiring policies of small-company executives. Chrissa Merron, Carole Cohn, and Sandy Folzer, friends who specialize in organizational development, helped me organize and conduct the focus group. Despite their crowded schedules, the following executives shared their views and an evening of their time with us:

Jack Asher, President, Asher Chocolates
Patrick Baldasare, President, The Response Center, Inc.
Carolyn Bennett, President, C. Bennett Scopes, Inc.
William Bromley, President, First Sterling Bank
Roy Carriker, Ph.D., President, Sermatech International, Inc.
Herbert Cohen, President, Resource Investment Group
Thomas Colman, Ph.D., COO, Scott Specialty Gases, Inc.
Patricia Foley, President, Creative Book Manufacturing
Lois Haber, President, Delaware Valley Financial Services, Inc.
Beverly Harper, President, Portfolio Associates
John Kowalski, General Manager, Technitrol, Inc.
Michael Levinson, President, Professional Training Services, Inc.
Paul Liberti, Ph.D., President, Immunicon Corp.
L. Martin Miller, Managing Partner, Cogen, Sklar, Levick & Co.
Claudia Pharis, President, Mentor Systems International, Inc.
Betsy Robinson, CEO, CYMA Corp.
Ron Rowe, President, J. W. Pepper & Son, Inc.
Al Rubin, Vice President, Cellular Headquarters, Inc.
Leslie Spero, Ph.D., Chairman, Strategic Management Group, Inc.
John Unangst, President, Franklin Mint Federal Credit Union
Ron Weber, President, Elastomeric Technologies Inc.
Jerry Young, President, The LAN Company

In addition, the following clients, small-company presidents, and executives also added their perspectives on the hiring process during personal interviews:

Katherine Anderson, Vice President, Right Associates
Barbara Andrew, CEO, Liberty Home Health
Maxine Ballen, Executive Director, and the staff of The Business Development and Training Center
Michael Baum, Executive Vice President, Francorp
Robert Benninghof, President, Bentech

Ellen Benson, Vice President, Human Resources, Common-
    wealth Federal Savings Bank
Ken Bentley, President, Diginet Communications Co.
Catherine W. Berheide, Associate Professor, Skidmore College
Frederic J. Beste, III, Managing Director, NEPA Management
    Corp.
Robert Bloom, President, Business Development Services, Inc.
Benjamin Brooks, President, Major Ben's Consulting Agency
Louis Buccelli, President, CME Conference Video
Francine Carb, Director of Marketing, Rabbit Software Corp.
Andre Carrington, Vice President, The Maxima Corp.
Della Clark, Manager, West Philadelphia Enterprise Center
Lisa Conte, President and CEO, Shaman Pharmaceuticals, Inc.
Mary Lou Cubbage, Career Counselor, West Chester Univer-
    sity
Sharon Dean, President, Corporate Factfinders
William Donaldson, CEO, nView Corp.
Linda Drake, President, TCI Telecall, Inc.
Nancy Drozdow, Principal, Center for Applied Research
Tom Drury, President, Syntellect Network Systems
William C. Dunkelberg, Dean, Temple University School of
    Business
Richard French II, President, Bagel Works, Inc.
Trish Hearn, Spokesperson, W. L. Gore, Associates
Marjorie Hill, Director, Kimberly Fukui and Susan Chang at
    the Ben Franklin Business Information Center
George Jenkins, General Partner, APA Fostin Pennsylvania
    Venture Capital Fund
Robert Kriebel, Senior Vice President, U.S. Bioscience
Aleda Loughman, President, Somat Corp.
Rebecca Maddox, President, Capital Rose, Inc.
Alan Segal, Managing Principal, Margolis & Co.
Will Messenger, Vice President, Advanced Metabolic Sys-
    tems, Inc.
Robert Molinari, President, AT Biochem, Inc.
Pam Murphy, Vice President, Greenwich Pharmaceuticals,
    Inc.

Joan Nowak, Vice President, Musselman Advertising

Tom and Kris O'Hara, owners, Alphagraphics

Sam Patterson, President, Shepard-Patterson and Associates

Bruce Phillips, Director of Economic Research, U.S. Small Business Administration

Karen Piazzi, Vice President, GMIS Inc.

Randy Pritzker, President, PBR Consulting Group

Marilyn Schaefer, Managing Editor, *Human Resource Executive* magazine

Larry Shapiro, President, The Center for Applied Psychology

Molly Shepard, President, Manchester, Inc.

Bernie Spain, CEO, Dollar Stores

John Swaren, Vice President, Knowledge Express Data Systems

Cathy Tisdale, Executive Director, American Red Cross of Lehigh Valley

John Wong, President, Apcot Corp.

Linda Yaffe, Director, Small Business Council, Greater Philadelphia Chamber of Commerce

To find out more about the experience of looking for a job, I turned to yet another network: the hundreds of people who attended my "How to Get a Job in a Small Company" seminars. I learned as much from them as they from me, and their stories were the spark for this book. I especially thank those who gave lengthy personal interviews, including Chuck Bonza, Ed Borkowski, Alan Brennecke, Robert Bryant, James Burget, Charles Chepak, Phil Clark, Rolf Dehmel, Joseph Gillies, Ronald Goldberg, Henry Hauptfuhrer IV, Richard Hough, Robin Mandell, David Needham, Michael O'Brien, Gary Schantz, and Sara Winckelman.

As my coauthor and I wrote each chapter, we sent copies to people in our network and asked them to read and critique the manuscript. They and others provided countless valuable insights. Among them were Caroline Glackin; Grant Greapentrog; Kathryn Keeler; Rick Mosenkis; Dewaine, Nancy, and Cindy Osman; Priscilla Rosenwald; and Susan Wood.

When we needed solitude to finish the book, Dewaine and Nancy Osman offered their beach house. My neighbors Alan and Libbie Soffer graciously let me intrude in their home to use their Apple computer and laser printer. My associate, Sonia Stamm, provided many valuable insights as our deadline approached.

My mentors, who encouraged me and guided me over the years and have been, in a sense, the four anchors of my career network, also deserve some of the credit for this book. Fred Beste, managing director, NEPA Management Corp., helped me enter the entrepreneurial world and bolstered my confidence. Mary Fahy, a therapist and career counselor, helped me through some difficult career choices. Harriet Hankin, president of The Consulting Group, was a colleague who became a friend and mentor at ARA Services. Dewaine Osman, a vice president at Unisys Corp., was a friend who became a mentor and colleague. All of them were there for me when I needed them the most.

Finally I would like to thank my family—my spirited and creative daughter, Tamra, who insisted that I push ahead with this project and "go for it" when my own resolve faltered; my father, who instilled in me the small-business spirit; and my mother, who taught me to think critically and complete whatever I start.

My partner in life, Stu Levy, was virtually a third coauthor of this book. He showed us how to structure the project and critiqued the chapters. He even carried the finished manuscript to the copy shop. He brought a wealth of information based on his firsthand knowledge of the world of manufacturing.

In my coauthor Kerry Pechter I found not only a writer but a trusted collaborator and cherished friend.

Kerry thanks the many people who agreed to share their occupational experiences. Special thanks to Joan and Edward Nowak, Tom and Kris O'Hara, Irvin Swider, Cindy Stains, and Marilyn Schaefer. Most of all, Kerry is grateful to his spouse, Lisa Higgins, for twelve years of unfailing love, understanding, and common sense. And he thanks his daughters, Hannah and Ariel, for their tender affection and for the drawings they brought to his office while he worked.

Foreword

William C. Dunkelberg

Dean of the School of Business and Management, Temple University
Author, *Small Business Optimism Index*, National Federation of
Independent Businesses

Do you remember your first job? I do. It was an entrepreneurial experience to say the least. In a year or two I built a multifaceted conglomerate that delivered an array of services including lawn care, child care, delivery, automotive services (e.g., I washed cars), and miscellaneous household services. The business never employed more than one person—my brother, who soon started his own enterprise in competition with me, adding an "incubator" function to my list of social achievements.

This effort was followed by a job at another small company, a nearby boat marina, which introduced me to sales, construction, engine repair, delivery (with a truck), customer relations, and a few other important functions beyond those I had already mastered working in my first firm. As I gained experience, I clearly became a more valuable employee, assuming more and more responsibility and managing more and more of the company's business. It was exciting. Each day confronted me with a very diverse set of activities, which challenged me, gave me confidence, and developed my skills.

My entry into the labor force is probably very typical of the experience of most Americans. Most of us begin our work life in a small firm, learning basic work-force and personal skills upon which we base our life work. Since I began working in my first small firm, I have started one company, been involved in the starting of several other ventures, and invested in many other entrepreneurs. As a professor of economics and Dean of the School of Business and Management at Temple University, I have studied small firms, written books about them, and developed new curricula with "total enterprise management" as the focus.

Small business is the R&D of the U.S. economy. It is dynamic and exciting. Large companies become bureaucratic "command" systems consisting of many "specialists" performing very narrow tasks with no vision about the mission and structure of the whole organization. Workers are "tracked" through the company in a series of specialized jobs. The closer one gets to the top, the less one really knows about the company, how it works, or what it does. Creativity is stifled by the narrow focus of each job and the immense scale of operations. The "big picture" people are so removed from the guts of the operation that they can't comprehend the problems and opportunities they face. It's like being mayor of Los Angeles or New York from a helicopter. It all looks pretty good from a distance (especially at night), and the major breakdowns are never anticipated.

Most employers in the United States are small. Ninety percent have fewer than 20 employees, and 98 percent have less than 100. Only 7,000 firms have over 500 employees. But the small companies are the most dynamic. If you want to be involved, like change and challenge, like having some control over the direction of your future, then growing small businesses provide the real employment opportunities. This is where things happen, where the new ideas are developed, and where tomorrow's Fortune 500 are being built. The employment opportunities among these firms are harder to find (they don't have large personnel departments), but they are more than worth the effort.

The opportunities for employment in the 1990s will not be at the "giants." What we have seen and learned in the past decade makes it clear that "flat" and "focused" organizations will succeed, that flexibility will be the key to profitability, that "niche" operations (a combination of specialization and marketing) will triumph over the "be everything to everyone" organizations, such as the conglomerates of the past. This all adds up to "small," or at least much smaller, firms.

Business schools are also working up to the changes in the structure of American industry. More and more classes on "entrepreneurship" are appearing in the course offerings. Even more important is the innovative work focused on "management of the total enterprise," an integrated set of courses and "real world" education that prepares students not to be specialists but to be managers with the diverse skills and the proper mind-set required for the new firms of the 1990s.

This book is the first guidebook for employment in this new industrial structure. It doesn't tell you how to dress or how to punctuate your resume. Rather it provides a fundamental perspective on the "lay of the land" of the employment opportunities among small firms in the 1990s. It provides the reader with the tools needed to develop an employment strategy for locating desirable jobs by identifying the differences between small- and large-firm management, needs, and employee-search processes. Job seekers from all backgrounds will find the perspective offered in this book helpful in designing their employment strategies and expanding their work opportunities. To survive in a new era, one must be aware of the nature of the environment being traversed. Don't go looking for a job in the nineties without this guidebook.

Manage Your Job Search Like a Small Business

This book is for those who would like to make a bigger splash in a smaller pond. In other words it is for anybody who harbors the dream of climbing from a stagnant middle-level job in a large organization to a senior-level job in a smaller company. Most specifically it is for the hundreds of thousands of people who have been squeezed by the recent "restructuring" of American business and who hope to achieve a more meaningful future—and more control over their destiny—in a smaller firm.

As an executive-search consultant and the creator of a popular seminar called "How to Get a Job in a Small Company," I've met thousands of such people. Some have been pushed into unwanted early retirement. Others have hit the "glass ceiling." Some are simply "plateaued" and wish they could recover the sense of accomplishment they used to feel at the end of the workday.

Their predicament, and their desire for a better understanding of the small-business job market, provided much of the motivation for this book. Their experiences in the small-business arena, as much as my own, were the source of the advice and information that you'll find here.

WHO SHOULD LOOK FOR A JOB IN A SMALL COMPANY?

• *People in their 40s or 50s who have been forced to retire early or have been laid off from large companies.* The "How to Get a Job in a Small Company" seminars are full of people from companies like Scott Paper, Du Pont, Unisys, and other major corporations that eliminated thousands of positions during the late 1980s and early 1990s. Some of these people received generous severance packages, golden parachutes, and free outplacement services. Others were simply led from the building by security guards.

• *Other newly unemployed white-collar, managerial, and professional workers.* Between 1990 and 1992, 300,000 white-collar workers lost their jobs, bringing the total number of unemployed managers and professionals in 1992 to about one million people and causing a 50 percent rise in the unemployment rate—from 2.1 percent two years earlier to 3.1 percent, according to the U.S. Department of Labor. Although the white-collar unemployment rate remains much lower than the blue-collar and minority unemployment rates, its rise has been sudden and dramatic.

• *People who are employed but plateaued.* According to books like Judith Bardwick's *The Plateauing Trap*, millions of Americans are going nowhere in their jobs. Many corporations, unable to promise advancement to as many people as they once could, have propped up morale and loyalty by encouraging employees to take enrichment courses or to transfer laterally within the company. But more people are realizing that they will never make vice president in a large corporation. For them, trying their luck at a small firm is preferable to languishing indefinitely at a large company.

• *People who have become disenchanted with life in large companies.* Some people in big companies would like to change jobs just to get away from the corporate politics, the constant reorganizations, and the resistance to change that characterizes many Fortune 500 companies today. Many of these people might find their need for greater autonomy more quickly fulfilled in a small company, where their professional management skills might be welcomed.

• *Former military personnel and workers who have been laid off from military contractors.* With the end of the Cold War, government spending on the military is being cut and head count in the armed forces is being reduced. Between 1993 and 1995 the Army alone is expected to shrink by 245,000 people. Between 1989 and September 1992, defense plants eliminated 300,000 jobs. An estimated 20 percent of the nation's engineers and scientists are employed under military contracts.

• *Recent college or graduate-school graduates.* College graduates have also been affected by the corporate-downsizing trend. Large companies are not hiring as many people, and not as many are sending recruiters to college campuses. Small companies rarely send recruiters, but they are hiring, and often welcome the fresh information and energy that recent college graduates offer.

• *Women, minorities, and older people.* By the year 2000 this group will comprise a majority of the American work force, and large companies won't have room to accommodate them. More and more women are starting their own small businesses, often because they've hit a "glass ceiling" that prevents them from rising to upper management. As they do, they'll be inclined to hire other women and to promote them to positions of authority. The same goes for members of minority groups.

• *People who don't have the fanciest of credentials.* Large organizations usually look for people who have gone to the right schools, had the right jobs with the right companies, and had their tickets punched at all the right places. But such people represent only a small percentage of all job seekers. There are lots of other talented people with diverse credentials, and they will find kindred spirits among the many fiercely individualistic, self-made people who own and operate small businesses.

HOW THIS BOOK WILL HELP YOU FIND A JOB IN A SMALL COMPANY

A Big Fish in a Small Pond will show you how to understand and penetrate the small-business market. The first section of the book will familiarize you with the small-business culture. It will also give you a sense of what jobs in small companies are like. In brief, chapters One through Six discuss:

- *The various types of small businesses.* Not all small businesses are alike. They differ in industry, type of ownership, and stages of development.
- *The differences between small and large companies.* Large companies tend to behave like armies, while small companies behave like families. The smaller the company, the more family-like it will be.
- *The needs and wants of the small-company CEO or president.* The three things a small-company "bullfrog" needs to know about you before he or she will hire you.
- *The emergence of women-owned businesses.* Women are starting businesses at twice the rate of men, and there are important differences in the management styles they practice.
- *The different types of small-company presidents.* This chapter will help you predict the personality and needs of a prospective employer by the type of company he or she runs.
- *What small-company managers really do.* Two jobs, one in a big company and another in a small company, may carry the same title. But that's not half the story.

The second section of the book will show you how to customize traditional job-search techniques for the small-business market. Your guiding principle, which I emphasize in my seminar, should be this: *To find the right job in a small business, you must manage your job search as though IT were a small business.* Chapters Seven through Twelve will enable you to do that, by showing you how to:

- *Understand your skills, abilities, and preferences.* Like a marketer analyzing a product, you must become intimately familiar with your own features, functions, and benefits before you can hope to sell yourself to a customer.
- *Determine whether you have the right stuff for small business.* Anyone can work in a small company, but not everyone can thrive in one. Find out if you have any or all of the ten traits needed for success in small business.
- *Network your way into the small-business market.* Small-business people are more likely to hire new managers through their personal network. This chapter reveals the "Zen" of networking.
- *Gather information about the small-company job market.* Public libraries and computer data bases have tons of well-indexed and accessible information about the small companies in your industry and geographical target area.
- *Customize your resume and cover letter for a small company.* Resumes are one of the necessary evils of your job search. The resume that works fine in a corporate job search may backfire in a small-company search.
- *Interview with a small-company executive.* Small-company "bullfrogs" will ask these questions: Can you add value to their company, do you understand the world of small business, and will you be easy to work with?

A Big Splash in a Small Pond is based on everything I've learned from years of helping thousands of people find good jobs at small companies. This book will help you understand small companies, locate them, and get inside them. I hope it will help you ride the crest of the wave of restructuring and downsizing that has created such turbulence in the American job market in recent years.

That turbulence, for better or worse, will continue to dominate the working world for the foreseeable future. Most of us will switch jobs and even careers several times in our lives. The organizations we work in are likely to be smaller, more maneuverable, and less predictable than the ones our elders worked in. Our only sense of security will come from knowing how to apply our talents and experience to fresh situations, and in our ability to manage our careers like successful small businesses. This book will furnish you with the tools to do that.

Why Look for a Job in a Small Company?

Small business in America has grown up.

When most of us were children, there were really only two kinds of companies in the United States. On one side of town, usually between the river and the railroad tracks, were the big industrial companies that provided most of the jobs. If you lived in Detroit, it was General Motors, Chrysler, and Ford. If you lived in San Francisco, it was Kaiser Aluminum and Lockheed. If you lived in Allentown, it was Mack Truck and Bethlehem Steel. Those were the companies with the most jobs to offer and the highest salaries to pay.

Meanwhile, down on Main Street, there were the small businesses that catered to personal needs—the shoe stores, the five-and-dimes, the doctors' offices, the attorneys' offices, the movie theaters, and the drugstores. These storefront operations employed relatively few people, and, except for the medical and law practices, paid relatively low wages.

Most men aspired to work for the large companies because that's where the money was. (Women were still concentrated in nursing, teaching, and homemaking.) Those who didn't work for the big firms sought job security in the fire department, the post office, or the school system. But unless your family owned a small business, you didn't set your sights on working in one. The rewards were too slim. Small business just wasn't sexy.

THE EMERGENCE OF THE DYNAMIC SMALL BUSINESS

But then the economic landscape in the United States shifted. The change started during the 1970s with the rising price of foreign oil and the resurgence of competition from industrial nations in Europe and Asia. It was pushed ahead in the 1980s by the emergence of high-technology industries and the feverish downsizing trend among big companies, who found that bigger wasn't always better. Recent books such as *The Work of Nations*, by Robert Reich, the U.S. Secretary of Labor in the Clinton administration; *Job Creation in America*, by David L. Birch; and *From the Ground Up*, by John Case, of *Inc.* magazine; have explained these changes in detail.

All of these factors helped create the right conditions for a new business genre: the high-growth small company. By that I mean any of the hundreds of thousands of exciting small companies, many of them based on breakthrough products in the computer, telecommunications, and biomedical fields, that have sprung up around the country during the last 20 years. These small (under 100 employees, for the most part) and highly maneuverable firms have proven in many cases to be better equipped than large corporations for capitalizing on rapid changes in the global marketplace as well as in the laboratory. Most importantly, they are said to be responsible for 80 percent of the job growth in America.

WHY LOOK FOR A JOB IN A SMALL HIGH-GROWTH COMPANY?

Here are six good reasons for turning your attention to the small company job market:

- *Most American companies are small.* Of the 20 million companies in the United States, only about 4,000 of them have more than 500 employees. There are about 14 million sole proprietorships, most of them too small to accommodate many new employees. There are two million partnerships. That leaves about four million small corporations. Of those corporations, according to David Birch of Cognetics, Inc., in Cambridge, MA, about 650,000 are actually growing at a high rate. He calls these companies the "gazelles" of the marketplace.
- *Most of the new jobs in the United States are created by small, growing companies.* During recessions, when large companies retreat like glaciers after an ice age, small businesses create virtually all the new jobs. "Domestic, dynamic small high-technology companies contributed almost four times their expected share of new jobs" during the 1980s, says the Small Business Administration (SBA), and that trend is expected to continue in the nineties.
- *Outplaced managers are finding jobs at smaller companies.* Although 90 percent of those who receive outplacement counseling come from large corporations, fewer than half go back into similar organizations. According to Right Associates, the national outplacement firm, 54 percent of their clients are hired by companies with fewer than 500 employees. Manchester Career Counseling Inc., a northeast firm, has estimated that about two-thirds of outplaced executives find jobs at companies smaller than the ones they left.
- *Small companies adapt well to today's international competition.* Although large companies, such as Sony and Apple, have the budgets needed to compete globally, smaller, more maneuverable companies can often respond better to rapidly changing international markets. According to the SBA, "in-

ternational pressures have resulted in shorter product cycles; in this environment, demand shifts before economies of scale are exhausted. And small firms are better able to respond to these shifts in demand."

• *Corporate America is "outsourcing."* Large companies are buying specialized products and services from small, independent suppliers instead of producing them in-house. In 1992 one-third of *Inc.* magazine's 500 fastest-growing small private American companies had a strategic alliance with a large company. Johnson & Johnson, for instance, relies on small California biotech firms for some of its basic research. Du Pont uses small consulting firms to show its computer department how to switch from mainframes to new client-server technology. Some of these companies are run by former employees of the large companies.

• *Large corporations are slimming down.* Many euphemisms have been coined to describe this trend—"outplacement," "right-sizing," "organizational flattening," "delayering," and "reengineering," for instance—but it amounts to the same thing: Large companies, particularly manufacturing companies, are shrinking.

"America's five hundred largest companies failed to create a single net new job between 1975 and 1990, their share of the civilian labor force dropping from seventeen percent to less than ten percent," wrote Robert Reich. And not just blue-collar workers and older workers are losing jobs. According to *Workplace Trends,* a newsletter, during the first seven months of 1992, an average of 1,674 jobs on corporate staffs were cut every day, adding up to a projected 350,000 to 400,000 lost jobs for the year.

Although some large companies, such as Wal-Mart and Microsoft, *added* tens of thousands of employees during the 1980s, industrial firms such as GM and IBM *eliminated* tens of thousands of jobs. They did so to take advantage of cheap labor overseas, or to reduce their debt, or to eliminate unprofitable lines of business. The result was that employment at the Fortune 500 fell by 3.7 million jobs between 1979 and 1989, from 16.2 million workers to only 12.5 million.

TODAY'S JOB MARKET IS 40 PERCENT MORE TURBULENT

In the broadest sense this book is for almost anyone who's been affected by the historical trends that are transforming the American economy.

The job market is increasingly unpredictable for many of us, who find ourselves in an occupational game of musical chairs in which more and more of us will spend less and less time at any single job.

Americans now change jobs, on average, once every three and a half years. According to the SBA, between 1976 and 1984, 84.5 million people changed jobs. Since the mid-1980s, in fact, the job market has become 40 percent more turbulent than in the previous decade as jobs have appeared and disappeared in a faster cycle than ever. Today one in five workers leaves his or her job each year. And Americans are not only changing jobs more often, they're changing careers more often. We used to average a career change every ten years, says Birch. Today one American in ten changes careers *every* year.

"Job security," writes Birch, "in the traditional sense of performing a function at a particular place over a long period, is less common today than it once was. . . . Gold watches will still be given to employees with long service to the firm, but there will be fewer presented in the future."

THE MERITS OF SMALL VERSUS LARGE

Not every small company, of course, belongs to the category of promising, high-growth gazelles. The majority of small companies remain in the low-growth, mom-and-pop category.

A recent book, *Employers Large and Small*, by Charles Brown, James Hamilton, and James Medoff, demonstrates that the wages, benefits, job security, and overall levels of job satisfaction in small companies are, *on average*, significantly lower than at large companies. They point out that while small businesses may account for most of the net job growth in the United States, small businesses also fail at a high rate.

But the purpose of this book is to help you find a job in one of the above-average small companies. Economists such as William Dunkelberg, dean of the Temple University business school, have found that about one in ten new companies breaks out of the pack by its third year and establishes itself as a high-growth company. That means there are hundreds of thousands of small *growing* companies where compensation and benefits are likely to be as good as or better than at large companies in the same industry. Those should be your target companies.

In my own career I grew up in a family that owned a small business, and I've worked in academia, nonprofit organizations, and big business. But in the end I returned to my roots in small business. What brought me back was a sense that small companies can provide the best environment for someone who's a bit of a nonconformist, who has a natural creative bent, and who wants to feel in command of his or her own destiny. In other words, someone who wants to be a big fish in a small pond.

Understanding the Small-Business Job Market

To find a job in the small-business job market, you need to know what life in a small company is like. As they said in the Broadway classic *The Music Man*, "You've got to know the territory."

For that reason the first half of this book is devoted to the characteristics of small companies. Those readers who can't wait to read about the technical nuts and bolts of a small-company job search are welcome to flip ahead to Part Two of this book. But in the long run, I believe, you will save days or weeks or even years by reading Part One first.

Why? Because the better you understand the familylike work culture and the daily pressures of small companies, the better equipped you will be to decide: (a) whether you possess the blend of versatility and independence that small companies demand; and (b) what type of small company you'd fit best in.

Part One will help you:

- Understand that not all small companies are alike
- Appreciate the differences between large and small companies
- Become sensitive to the way small-business owners think
- Recognize how small-business CEOs vary in temperament and style
- Interpret the meaning of job titles in small companies

The smaller the company of course, the less it will resemble a large corporation. By the same token, as little businesses grow, they gradually acquire the stabilizing hierarchies and formal policies that characterize larger companies.

If you've worked only at large companies, the characteristics of small companies might surprise you. Day-to-day cash-flow concerns will be more intense, but your chances of getting equity in the company might be greater. Both your triumphs and your mistakes will be noticed more. You'll probably end up managing fewer people, but your responsibilities will probably grow.

Since the cultures of small companies tend to be less predictable than the standardized cultures of big ones, you'll have to probe more deeply, and conduct more due-diligence research, to assess the terrain of any particular small company. That means finding out who owns and runs it, what stage of growth it's in, and whether it's in an industry with growth potential.

In a small company you'll rub shoulders with the CEO much more frequently than you would at a large company. For that reason the positive chemistry that develops—or fails to develop—between you and the CEO will have much greater impact on the quality of your working life than it would in a big firm.

The small-company job market might seem like a dense, impenetrable thicket at first. After all, the United States is home to millions of small firms and only a few thousand large ones. But the sheer multiplicity of small companies, and the fact that new small companies are born every day, almost guarantees that if you search diligently, you'll eventually find a "perfect fit."

When you've finished Part One, you should have a clearer sense of how well suited you'd be to a small company. At that point you'll also be better prepared to understand and use the material in Part Two. Even if you've worked in small companies before, the material in the first section might offer you new insights into the dynamics of small firms and perhaps, in retrospect, help you better understand your experiences there.

CHAPTER ONE

Small Businesses, Like Fish, Come in All Shapes and Sizes

The expression *small business* gets bandied about so much that it begins to lose all meaning. To an IBM executive, a small business is a $120 million software vendor that employs 1,000 people. To the president of a small-town chamber of commerce, a small business is the pet shop that just opened downtown and employs three people: the founder, his son-in-law, and their part-time assistant.

The truth is, small businesses, like species of fish, come in all shapes and sizes. There are retail, high-tech, manufacturing, and business-service companies. There are companies run by entrepreneurs, by families, and by professional managers. There are venture-backed firms, publicly traded firms, and firms that are owned by major companies or holding companies.

Each type of business has its own peculiar employment needs and culture. Some companies have a formal, hierarchical, or even dictatorial culture. Others have a democratic, collegial culture. Very small businesses may generate enough cash to enrich the owner and no one else, while high-growth, public small businesses may make the entire management team into a millionaires' club.

For the person who must search through the highly segmented small-business market for a high-paying job, understanding these differences is crucial. You can't conduct an efficient job search if your efforts are scattered indiscriminately across the small-business spectrum. You must focus your efforts on a specific band of the small-business job market. To do that, you must understand the ways in which small businesses differ from one another.

YOU MUST BECOME A "HEADHUNTER"

As a so-called headhunter (or, more politely, an executive recruiter), I've observed this problem from the point of view of the small-company CEOs. I know how difficult it is for them to find a new engineer or CFO. In fact they pay executive recruiters like myself a great deal of money to spare them the trouble of combing the entire United States for a candidate with exactly the right skills and industry experience. My job is to understand my client's needs clearly and then to evaluate each potential candidate with those needs in mind.

You must do the same thing in reverse when you "headhunt" a small company that will meet your needs. You must assess your own requirements and then evaluate each potential employer with those needs in mind. How do you do that? By finding out how each prospective employer differs from the rest. Small companies usually differ in the following ways:

• *Industry.* Small companies can be found in almost any industry. The fastest-growing industries are computers, telecommunications, health care, international trade, business services, and others. But small companies have found profitability in any field, from custom apparel to specialty coffees.

• *Types of ownership and management.* Small companies can be owned by a family, a holding company, a large corporation, its employees, or by a group of investors. They may be privately held, publicly held, or financed by venture capital. The company might be operated by the owner, by a group of family members, or by a hired professional manager.

• *Stages of development.* Growing companies, not unlike people, progress through a series of distinct stages of development. Those stages are called courtship, infancy, adolescence, and prime.

Looking for the right small company is a little like searching for dinosaur bones. You have to know where to look and you have to know how to recognize and classify what you find. Aside from familiarizing you with the various types of small companies, the following information will help you decide what kind of small business you'd like to work in (and thereby show you where to focus your time and energy), and it will help you classify the small companies that come to your attention during your search. To paraphrase Henry David Thoreau, you must "systematize, systematize, systematize!"

WHAT INDUSTRY IS IT IN?

In evaluating a potential employer, you first need to find out which industry it is in. Then you need to find out whether that industry is growing, or if the company is growing despite being in a low-growth industry.

High-growth industries

In the United States today, some industries are growing much more quickly than others. If you're already in one of the following high-growth industries, you should probably stay in it. If you're

Hot Industries Dominated by Small Business

The following industries, in each of which at least 60 percent of the employees worked in businesses with fewer than 500 employees, produced the following numbers of new jobs between September 1990 and September 1991, according to the U.S. Small Business Administration's Office of Advocacy:

Nursing and personal-care facilities	96,000
Outpatient-care facilities	39,300
Residential care	52,300
Offices of physicians	74,900
Individual and family services	26,000
Non-health-care growth areas:	
Computer and data processing services	54,000
Mailing, reproduction, and stenographic services	21,000
Engineering and management services	27,200
Total	390,700

switching careers, consider repackaging your marketing, financial, or organizational skills so that you can transfer into one of them.

Computers and telecommunications. Cellular-telephone companies, computer-systems integration firms, custom-software companies, computer leasing firms, 900-phone-number services, computer peripheral manufacturers, data-base distributors—these are among the dozens of specialized fields in which many of the young, fast-growing *Inc.* Magazine 500 companies, for instance, can be found.

In fact the small but volatile high-tech segment has generated new jobs at four times the rate of other business sectors since as far back as the mid-1970s, according to the Small Business Administration. By the early 1990s new high-tech firms were forming at the rate of 14 percent per year, about twice the rate of U.S. industry as a whole.

"'Brainy" and "intense" are two ways to describe the culture at small high-tech companies. Most of the managers will have advanced science or engineering degrees. In the heady, fast-paced high-tech market, new products have a maximum shelf life of 18 months, so the demand for innovation is constant. These companies will offer high salaries to compete for top talent. Compensation may be a blend of equity and cash, with bonuses tied to performance.

Many high-tech firms enter the world either as corporate spin-offs, as joint ventures with large firms, or as suppliers to large firms. The financially healthiest ones usually maintain symbiotic relationships with large corporations. High-tech CEOs usually look for a close fit between the job seeker's credentials and their needs. Even the sales reps at these firms often have MBAs and undergraduate degrees in science.

Often early-stage high-tech companies that are developing new technologies and new products can be located through state-sponsored funding programs and in the business incubators or "science parks" that can be found near major universities.

Health care and biotech. Health care companies outperformed the rest of the economy in the late 1980s and early 1990s, largely because health care spending continued to rise. Three million new health care jobs are expected to be created between 1992 and 2000. Nursing homes, doctors' offices, and pharmaceutical companies will all add hundreds of thousands of jobs as the U.S. population ages. Many of those positions will pay low wages, while others will require specialized medical skills. But nursing homes and large medical practices also need accountants, marketing managers, and administrators.

Biotechnology firms offer many new opportunities for those with sophisticated skills. One MBA recently left McKinsey & Co., the large management consulting firm, to join a tiny company in Massachusetts that markets a new method for administering insulin to diabetes sufferers. He took a pay cut in return for an equity stake, a vice president's title, and "a chance to make a difference."

"At McKinsey you're always advising managers and putting yourself in their shoes. And everybody is always talking about starting or running a company. So when I got the opportunity, I took it," he says. He "made a difference" by convincing the CEO to charge for the new product on a per-patient basis rather than simply selling the devices outright to doctors. He's one of only three managers in a 10-person company that has high hopes of employing 500 people within four years.

International business. As global communications and transportation systems have shrunk the world, more small American companies are looking to foreign markets to increase their sales. In 1987, the latest year for which figures were available, 130,000 U.S. companies sent at least one shipment overseas. The most exciting opportunities are in telecommunications, medical lasers and other instruments, and computer hardware and software.

One Virginia-based firm makes and sells a device that projects images from a computer display onto a wall or screen for sales or educational presentations. With sales doubling to $32 million between 1991 and 1992, the firm now has 89 employees and is in its second stage, having gone public and installed formal controls and policies. "We're about halfway between being a gangly teenager and an adult," says the president, a 36-year-old former MIS manager who landed his job through a personal contact on the board of directors.

Executives in international companies must be more cosmopolitan than their domestic counterparts. As marketers they must know how to adapt a product to the needs, tastes, laws, or customs of non-Americans. They must also be adept at cross-cultural communications and negotiations and recognize that Japanese, German, and Latin American customers use their own characteristic styles of doing business.

Salaries at international companies are on average 17 percent higher than at domestic companies, one survey has shown. (That statistic may merely reflect the high costs of expatriate programs.) Compensation ranges widely, from $95,000 (plus stock options) for the president of the company mentioned above, to $600,000 for a vice president and partner of a fast-growing, Illinois-based maker of modems for businesses worldwide.

Business services. Large companies are increasingly "ordering out" for many of the business services that they once produced in-house—a practice widely known as outsourcing. Data processing services, advertising, public relations, management consulting, computer programming, and temporary office help are increasingly purchased from outside contractors. This trend has stimulated growth among small companies in those fields and created many new jobs.

Salaries for those in business services are often much higher than for services in general. Providers of professional services such as legal, accounting, and engineering services command some of the highest salaries. The newer the company, the more likely it is that compensation will be based primarily on performance. A typical business-service company requires people who are not only expert in their field but who also must have a flair for selling and interacting smoothly with clients.

As the economy weakened in the late 1980s, businesses services actually benefited. Between 1982 and 1987, according to the most recent Census of Service Industries, both receipts and payroll in business services doubled. By the end of the 1980s a lot of high-flying real estate, investment, and insurance firms had suddenly come down to earth. But the survival rate of business-service firms nearly doubled.

High-growth companies in low-growth industries

With all the attention focused on high-tech companies, it's easy to forget that many new jobs have been created by the innovative companies that have breathed new life into old industries. No one knew that millions of dollars were waiting to be churned out in the ice-cream industry before Häagen-Dazs and Ben & Jerry's Homemade, Inc. came along. Until a little company named Celestial Seasonings popped up in Colorado, no one knew there was a gold mine in herbal tea. The same could be said for

How to Create a Small-Company Qualification Chart

As a headhunter I'm constantly making lists of companies that I'm targeting for business purposes. It's a prospect qualification tool that brings together the bits of vital information I need about each one of them.

For your purposes, and for the purpose of your job search, you need to create a list of companies that interest you, along with any information, such as industry, stage, type of ownership, as well as name of principal contact, size, and whatever additional information (do they export? what is their year-to-year growth rate? name of accounting firm?) that might help you keep them straight in your mind. It's all part of systematizing your job search so that you can run it like a small business.

COMPANY:	#1	#2	#3	#4	#5
Industry					
Stage					
Ownership					
Gross Sales					
Employees					
Contact					
Phone #					
Comments					

Smith & Hawken with their mail-order garden-tool business, or for Starbucks, the Seattle-based marketer of gourmet coffees. These companies started small but didn't stay that way for long. The lesson: Don't overlook good companies that happen to be in mature industries.

Not-for-profit agencies and institutions

Not-for-profit agencies, such as social service, cultural, and educational institutions, are an often-overlooked source of worthwhile management jobs. Such agencies need experienced managers who can handle large budgets and staffs and know how to raise money.

The director of a chapter of the American Red Cross in a small city, for instance, might have to manage a budget of over $1 million and work harmoniously with a staff of 25 or 30 people, hundreds of volunteers, and a board of directors. "We have the additional burden of marketing intangible services, which makes it hard to generate cash. That means we're constantly scrambling for grants. You're working harder to create revenue streams than if you had a hard product with a price tag on it," says one Red Cross chapter director.

Not-for-profits have traditionally paid less than companies in the private sector, largely because they're dependent on public funds and donations for their income. But salaries are rising at the larger social service organizations as they strive to compete for skilled managers. As in other small businesses, managers of not-for-profits must know how to stretch a dollar and often barter for what they need.

Who owns it? who runs it?

You can tell a lot about a company by finding out who owns it and who runs it. Some small firms are owned and led by the people—the entrepreneurs, family, partners, scientists, or former corporate executives—who founded them. Others are run by professional managers who have been brought in specifically to run the company. Each form of ownership has its own particular characteristics.

The family-owned company

Millions of people work for family-owned companies. Figures vary, but it's been estimated that more than *80 percent* of all businesses in the United States are operated, controlled, or owned by families. Together they account for roughly half the U.S. gross national product. How could that be? Over 90 percent of all U.S. businesses are very small, and most very small companies are run by members of an extended family. But family businesses range in size from the classic mom-and-pop corner grocery to corporations like Campbell's Soup, Johnson's Wax, Levi Strauss, and Marriott Corp.

Many family firms have a genuinely familylike culture that embraces even nonfamily members. At one small publishing house, for instance, the family hosted an annual clambake at the chairman's home every summer, and clerks could talk to vice presidents over lunch in the corporate dining room. Employees were on a first-name basis with the chairman and his wife. Most of the executives—the president and all but one of the vice presidents—were nonfamily members.

In many family businesses, however, the members of the family rank first, and the opinions of nonrelatives carry less weight. One CFO at a small auto-parts manufacturer has unpleasant memories of his brief turn as V.P. of finance at a firm run by a father and three sons. The CFO soon found out that decisions made in the office were often unmade over the family dinner table. "We'd make a decision at a meeting on Friday," he said, "and on Sunday the three sons would sit down to dinner with mom and dad and change our decision."

The benefits of working in a family business, says Nancy Drozdow, Ph.D., the director of the family-business practice at the Center for Applied Research, Inc., in Philadelphia, are that families usually look far ahead and anticipate the needs of coming generations. They invest for the long term rather than the short. Unlike venture-backed companies, they're not created merely to be fattened and sold. Since in many cases their personal reputation is so closely associated with their product, they're more quality-conscious.

Optimal candidate: Since any business, at any stage, and in any industry can be a family business, it's difficult to generalize about who would fit in best in this type of company. A candidate for a job in a family company should recognize that the top positions may be reserved for family members.

The founder-owned, founder-led small company

This type of firm is usually started by an individual or a partnership who had an idea for a new product or service and decided to start a business. Architectural, legal firms, and other consulting firms belong to this category, as well as small companies that were subsidiaries of a large company until a group of engineers or managers pooled their funds and bought them out. Entrepreneurial firms are usually predicated on a new drug, a better piece of software, or simply a new twist on an old concept.

One of the "new twist" variety is Bagel Works, Inc. Started at the end of the 1980s by four socially conscious University of Vermont graduates who wanted to do for bagels what Ben & Jerry's did with ice cream, Bagel Works financed its first bakery in Manchester, Vermont, with money borrowed from friends and the Small Business Administration.

Eighteen months later the partners opened a second store in Portland, Maine, and a year after that a store in Keene, New Hampshire. Sales rose from $250,000 to $1.5 million in three years, and the founders, who started out kneading the dough and waiting on customers themselves, soon graduated to problems such as administration and strategic planning.

Companies like Bagel Works can be exhilarating to work for. "When a company is growing and striving for its first $1 million in sales, it can be the most exciting kind of environment to be in. There's no bigger high than when you're building a culture, putting the right people in place, and getting stock options," says one CFO who has worked for three entrepreneurial firms.

Often these companies don't have cultures; they assume the personalities of their owners. Working in one is like crewing on an America's Cup racing yacht, where each person has a critical role to play, everybody is committed to a single goal, and all are directed by the strong-willed individual who brought the shipwright and the investors and the crew together in the first place.

"Highly successful entrepreneurs often have an extreme need for recognition, power, independence, and the satisfaction of creating something wholly their own," adds Steven Solomon in *Small Business USA*. "Most are highly competitive and see only two places to finish—first and last. Many draw no distinction between work and play. They are often colorful, eccentric, and sometimes rebellious personalities who have trouble with authority figures of all sorts."

Optimal candidate: somebody who can work with a strong, charismatic—and sometimes even eccentric—personality with a minimum of friction; who brings skills to the company that the original owners do not have; and who does not need the status that goes with working for a large, prestigious firm. Native talent and compatibility with the owner are the most important prerequisites for success at this type of company.

The venture-backed or publicly owned, professionally led small firm

Venture-backed firms can be the most exciting small businesses to work in. For managers who want to create new products, open up new markets, and get a chance to own equity that could potentially make them millionaires, venture-backed firms are the way to go.

Typically, venture-backed firms are started by an inventor or entrepreneur who, needing cash to finance growth, has sold much of the equity in his company to a group of investors. The investors hope to make the company grow rapidly and sell it at a large profit, either to other investors or to the public through a stock offering. Consequently the investors demand high-performance and quick results from the managers they hire.

Sometimes these businesses can take off like a rocket. A few years ago a start-up company named Conner Peripherals, just one of many wannabe disk-drive makers in Silicon Valley, was scrounging for venture capital. When its founders finally found funding, they developed a very tiny, shockproof disk drive that quickly became the standard for the new wave of laptop and other portable computers made in the United States and Asia. Conner, Inc. now has over a billion dollars in international sales.

Venture-backed companies make up only a tiny percentage of all companies, but they are rich sources of professional jobs. According to a 1992 survey by Coopers and Lybrand and Venture Economics, venture-backed high-tech companies created 58,000 highly skilled jobs in the United States between 1985 and 1990. Half of the jobs in a typical venture-backed company require graduate degrees. In the average American company, only 15 percent of the jobs require professional training, according to a 1991 U.S. Bureau of Labor Statistics report.

Optimal candidate: As one executive put it, people with the *Star Trek* mentality; those who "dare to go where no earthling has gone before." Corporate executives who are looking for a challenge and technically sophisticated people with applicable industry experience should definitely apply.

The small division or subsidiary of a large corporation

Business gurus predict that in the future even large companies will be broken down into smaller units that behave like efficient, entrepreneurial-minded small companies. The model for this company already exists today at places like W. L. Gore & Associates, the $500 million Delaware firm that was started by a former Du Pont scientist with a novel idea for making breathable, waterproof fabric out of Teflon fiber. It's called Gore-Tex.

Although W. L. Gore employs 5,000 workers worldwide, few if any of its plants are staffed by more than 200 people. Employees are called associates, and anyone who generates new ideas and demonstrates leadership can become a manager or sponsor.

"You can lead only if you develop a following," says one former Gore leader. "There are pockets of strong, authoritarian people, but the management style is fluid, and decision-making tends to be by consensus." Ad hoc task forces are formed to work on specific projects. Compensation is based on contribution to the bottom line, as determined by a peer committee.

Small units of big companies offer certain advantages. There's usually more opportunity for transfers and promotions. A big company also tends to be more financially stable than a small one. On the other hand, small divisions of large companies may find that their hands are tied by the parent company's policies or reporting requirements.

Optimal candidate: This type of small company offers the easiest possible transition for someone coming from a large company who needs stability and is accustomed to the structure and hierarchies of a large company.

The small company owned by a holding company

Much the same can be said for small companies that have been purchased by large holding companies. These holding companies act much like absentee landlords. As long as the business remains profitable, they don't normally try to micromanage their companies.

One such company is a 12-person, $2.5 million manufacturing firm that designs and produces handrails and other metal fixtures for city buses and subway cars. Established in 1880, the company's culture, like that of other small metal-bending shops, is gritty and informal. In 1985 it was purchased by an investor group located in a distant city, but the president still enjoys a great deal of freedom. If he wants to give an employee $1,000 to help with night-school tuition, or promote an energetic part-time janitorial worker to head of shipping, he can do that.

Holding companies can usually afford to pay big-company

salaries in a small-company setting. One sales manager, recently hired by a $15 million Connecticut-based adhesives firm, found that its holding company could afford to pay him generously. To win the job, however, he had to sweat through four interviews at the subsidiary, two interviews at the holding-company headquarters in Chicago, and a 14-page written examination.

Optimal candidate: A manager who feels comfortable in the division of a large company and who is capable of working independently but also responding to the needs and demands of the holding company. This person should be cool enough to work with holding-company executives who do not understand the problems faced by the companies in their portfolio and who may hand down financial or personnel decisions that show no sensitivity to or understanding of the smaller company's needs.

STAGES OF GROWTH

Regardless of the type of ownership, all companies go through a similar series of growth stages. In fact a company might be likened to a fruit tree. The tree puts forth a flower (a money-making idea, let's say), which is pollinated or fertilized by a bee (an investor or customer). If the weather (market condition) is favorable, and if the tree is carefully watered, nourished, and pruned (managed well), it may bear fruit.

Ichak Adizes, Ph.D., in his 1988 book *Corporate Lifecycles*, chooses a different metaphor. He claims that companies usually find themselves in one of the following stages (though not always in the following order):

Courtship

During the courtship period a business exists merely as a gleam in the entrepreneur's eye. At this early stage nothing but the entrepreneur's pure obsessive belief in it is keeping his or her fragile idea alive. Anyone who joins a company during the courtship stage has to share that obsession and be willing to sacrifice time, money, and home life to make the venture a success.

"The motivation of a founder has to be transcendental," says Adizes. "It must exceed the narrow limits of immediate gain. The commitment cannot only be rational."

Optimal candidate: A person who knows the founder, has gained the founder's trust, and ideally has participated in the founding of the company. Family members and close friends are often the best candidates for companies in an embryonic stage.

Infancy

William Paley, the founder of the CBS radio and television networks, once remarked that he most enjoyed his company's early years, before both he and CBS became rich, famous, and powerful. Many people would agree with Paley that a company's infancy is its headiest time.

A company leaps from courtship to infancy when financing has been secured, a team has been assembled, and the first products are moving out the door. No policies or systems have yet been created, and the culture is egalitarian and collegial. Co-workers become closer to each other than they are to their own families. Every experience is new and therefore thrilling.

Some people prefer to work only in infant companies. One manager, a former executive at a $2.5 billion chemical company, sought out infant-stage companies who needed help in bringing new products to market. "What I bring to the party is strong commercialization skills," he says. "My job is to get the money in the right place at the right time."

Optimal candidate: People who are either near the beginning or near the end of their careers are the best candidates for jobs in infant companies. If you have nothing to lose by taking a chance on a fledgling firm, if you can go to work not knowing exactly how your skills will be used, and if you know that you're good but you need to find an employer who's willing to gamble on you, you might love working in an infant company.

Go-go

In the "go-go" stage, however, the company's early success has gone to its head, and a kind of overconfident giddiness sets in. Companies that are lucky enough to reach this stage are growing by leaps and bounds, and the cash flow exceeds everyone's expectations. The president may begin to think he has a Midas touch. A job applicant who interviews at a company in the go-go stage might even be hired on the spot, simply because the company needs new people so urgently.

But the job seeker should beware of the giddy, strap-on-your-helmet feeling that the president may try to infect you with. Many go-go companies are headed for a tumble. Eventually the president may try to diversify into a business he's not familiar with, and the company will experience a sobering crisis from which it may or may not recover.

Optimal candidate: If you're a thrill junkie, you'll love working in a go-go company. If you also need a high salary, go-go companies can afford to pay you. But beware: Go-go companies often take risks that can send them over the brink into financial failure. If you're a turnaround specialist who loves to manage crises, you might find a home at a go-go company that has begun to go over the brink and needs a steady hand to rescue it.

Adolescence

A young firm's adolescence is its most awkward stage. Typically a company in this stage is a divided camp. A war is going on between the original gang of technicians and inspired amateurs who started the company and a new group of professional, bean-counting managers that have been hired by the founder to implement systems and controls and to formalize the culture so that the early successes aren't frittered away.

Adolescence is characterized by palace intrigues and secret meetings. The tension eventually breaks when the founder chooses whether to back his old team or his new team. Either way someone will end up getting fired. Venture-backed firms can remain in adolescence for years as the investors keep juggling managers until they find a winning combination. But adolescence isn't all bad. It can be a time of excitement and accomplishment, with great opportunities for advancement.

Optimal candidate: People with high self-esteem, good people-skills, and a talent for bringing order out of chaos will succeed in adolescent companies. If you're a "fixer" who can keep your head above the fray and know how to introduce change gradually and diplomatically to people who resist it, an adolescent company might suit you.

Prime

A company reaches its "prime" when its managers have discovered a formula for success. They have established policies that will ensure the company's continued success. Overconfidence has cooled into wisdom. The company sets a budget and meets it, makes plans and carries them out, is proactive rather than reactive. The prime company's challenge is to stay in prime and not become too conservative or complacent to adapt to rapid changes in the marketplace.

Optimal candidates: To land a job at a prime company, you must have exactly the skills and credentials that the company is looking for. Prime companies hire very deliberately and selectively, often using executive recruiters.

Swimming Lessons

The information in this chapter will help you in two ways:

First, it will help you identify, *prior* to your job search, which type of company, stage of development, and industry you find most attractive. By narrowing your search down to certain categories—provisionally at least—you stand to save yourself months of hacking haphazardly through the jungles of small businesses. To find something, you have to know what you're looking for.

Second, the informal classification system described in this chapter will help you define and categorize the companies that you become aware of through newspaper ads, tips from your network contacts, magazine articles, and computerized data bases. You can use this system to answer the question: Does Company XYZ match the stage, ownership style, and industry that I'm looking for?

Obviously you will modify your goals during your job search, as you will throughout your career. But a systematic approach to the small-company market will help you distinguish the most desirable prospects from the less desirable prospects more quickly and thus enable you to find your dream job faster. Goals can't be reached until they can be visualized. As Lily Tomlin put it in *The Search for Intelligent Life in the Universe*, "I knew I always wanted to be somebody. I guess I should have been more specific."

Tips

⚡ Job seekers who have only known large corporations will be most comfortable in small companies that are subsidiaries of large companies or are managed by other former corporate executives.

⚡ Search out companies that are in the "go-go" stage. They hire at enormous rates in order to support their rapid (and sometimes undisciplined) growth.

⚡ As the medical industry comes under pressure to cut costs, small health care companies will need experienced financial managers, savvy marketing people, and customer-service experts to help them compete.

⚡ If you're switching from one industry to another, do your homework. Study the market, cultivate individuals in that industry whom you know or need to know, and find ways to apply your skills to that industry.

⚡ Business services offer opportunities for professionals who combine two skills: a thorough knowledge of their specialty and an ability to develop and nurture relationships with clients.

- Seek opportunities to visit small companies. Ask about their industry and markets, form of ownership, and stage of development. Get a sense of the culture and working environment.

CHAPTER TWO

Comparing Small-Company Ponds to Large Corporate Oceans

Small companies differ from large companies as dramatically as families differ from armies, as Hondas do from Cadillacs, as Republicans do from Democrats—or as ponds do from oceans. To extend our marine metaphor, a corporation resembles an ocean liner: difficult to maneuver, but very steady. By comparison a small company is akin to a 19-foot sloop in choppy waters off the coast of Nantucket: at the mercy of every sudden squall, but exciting as hell to sail in.

As one person who moved from GE Capital Mortgage Corp. to a small venture-financing firm put it, there are "five universes of difference" between large- and small-company cultures. And the greater the difference in size, the greater the contrast.

In the more formal culture of a large company, for instance, most employees couldn't imagine having direct access to the CEO. They usually earn higher salaries and enjoy more security, but that's changing, as the rash of downsizing, mergers, and industry shakeouts of the 1980s and 1990s have demonstrated. Behavior at large companies is usually dictated by time-honored policies.

Employees in small companies experience a more informal and much less predictable environment. Almost anyone can knock on the CEO's door. On the other hand, the CEO is more likely to have a quirky personality. Small-company workers need to be more versatile, independent, and decisive. Small companies have a higher mortality rate than large ones, but their high birth rate makes them a fertile source of opportunity.

DIFFERENCES IN THE TERMS OF EMPLOYMENT

More impressive title, less corporate name recognition

If you become a big fish in a small pond, your business card will be both more impressive, because of your loftier title, and less impressive, since few people will have heard of your company.

An entrepreneur who used to work for a major American toy maker often tells this story: whenever he was flying on business, he looked forward to the moment when the passenger sitting next to him would ask him where he worked. When he uttered his company's famous name, the stranger usually responded with a glow of envious admiration. How he loved to bask in that glow. Enjoyable as those experiences were, however, they didn't offset the frustration of being an anonymous middle manager lost in the bureaucratic forest of a large corporation.

Trade-offs in compensation and benefits

There's a broad range in the compensation and benefits that small companies offer. Depending on their industry, profitability, and growth potential, some small companies may offer salary-and-benefits packages comparable to those of large companies. Some offer generous stock-ownership plans to their employees. Others fail even to offer health benefits.

According to *Employers Large and Small* (Harvard University Press, 1992) by professors Brown, Hamilton, and Medoff, workers in small firms earn an average of 30 percent less than similar workers in large companies. Even when other factors are accounted for—such as the tendency for large companies to be located in metropolitan areas, where wages are generally higher—workers in large firms take home 10 to 15 percent more.

Nor do small companies, on the whole, offer comparable benefits. An estimated three-fourths of the working Americans who have no health insurance work in small companies, largely because small companies can't afford to insure them.

But small companies can be generous when they have to be. One CEO of a 50-employee pharmaceutical company intentionally adopted Johnson & Johnson's pay scale in order to compete with J&J in the labor market. Going J&J one better, he introduced a pay-for-performance and equity-distribution system that rewarded every employee for reaching his or her goals.

That same CEO recruited a 50-year-old Australian-born manager who had formerly run the Belgian and Korean operations for a large pharmaceutical company to manage the international sales of a new and controversial arthritis drug. The new manager received the same six-figure salary he earned at the large company, plus a hefty stock option.

Compensation packages at small companies are more likely to be open for negotiation. One sales representative was offered a job as a director of customer service for a small computer software company at $9,000 less than he'd made at a large firm. To offset the pay cut, he negotiated for two weeks' extra vacation, a four-day work week, and occasional afternoons off to coach his son's soccer team. One small-business owner helps his managers by compensating their spouses for the part-time administrative chores they perform at home.

More Davids than Goliaths

Small companies often offer havens for talented people who simply don't fit the corporate mold. They have no patience for playing politics. They are creative and iconoclastic. They have a David-versus-Goliath view of the corporate battlefield, with themselves cast as David.

One of my clients fits that description. He was born in a tough urban neighborhood and was the first member of his family to attend college. By his early forties, he was director of product development for a unit of a Fortune 500 company and was headed for vice presidency. But he hated it. He quit to run a small company where his principal job is raising venture capital. He's out to "beat the big guys" at their own game, and he works 15 hours a day doing it.

DAY-TO-DAY DIFFERENCES IN SMALL-BUSINESS CULTURE

You'll see the fruits of your labor every day

People in small companies are more likely to feel that they've completed something during the course of the day. One executive, who had worked at Hercules, a $2.5 billion chemical company, before moving to a start-up company that markets a new, high-tech paging device for doctors, described the satisfaction that came from seeing his ideas put into action and then watching the positive—or even negative—reaction they produced.

"We're in the early stages of commercialization, and we have just a handful of customers," he says, "but there's no question that when they send us checks for big chunks of money or give us a referral, we know that it's because of the work that we personally did. It wasn't because of the reputation of the company or a famous brand name. There's no equivocation: we earned it. The results are yours, be they good or bad, and even bad results can be satisfying because they're yours.

"In a small company," he adds, "your time is spent much

more focusing on the external things, on making the external market respond to you. In a large company you spend much more time working with people internally, building a consensus to get what you want, working with staff groups and committees. The difference is that in a small company your energy is focused outward. And that's a healthy difference."

Others agree. "It's easier to see what your contribution is," says one person who joined an international start-up after years with a large company. "When I helped start my company's small European operation, I set up the benefit plan, helped hire people, went on sales calls with the engineers. In a big company you get into a staff function where you do your little piece of the puzzle, but you can't see the effect of your contribution."

Greater visibility in a small firm

There's no question that at a small company each person stands out more. Recognition for a job well done comes more quickly and directly. At the same time the pressure to perform is also more direct. Most small businesses operate in close quarters, where the inner workings of the business are visible to all.

Some people prefer the anonymity of a large company. "I've had employees here at Hewlett-Packard," says one former HP manager, who said to me, 'Don't ask for my initiative. I don't want to climb the ladder. What I really like doing is raising orchids.' They come in at eight and leave at five and observe the rituals and enjoy the anonymity." That rarely happens at a small company.

Others need the anonymity of a large corporation. An accountant who works for one of my clients worked best when he was alone. He functioned just fine as an obscure number cruncher in a large service organization, but problems cropped up when he took a job as a controller at a small firm that installed local area network systems, or LANs. He had to work shoulder-to-shoulder with the president, who assigned him to personnel chores that required even more human contact. Rather than fire him, the president assigned him to work part-time at home.

Fewer meetings, faster decisions

The number of formal meetings seems to be directly proportional to a company's size. The larger the company, the greater the tendency to schedule large meetings with planned agendas. Given the large numbers of people needed to make decisions at large firms, these meetings are often unavoidable. But the handful of managers at small companies find it more convenient to meet in the hallway, at a deli, or at home.

"If you can't make the decision yourself," said one manager, "then you just get three or four people in a room and within fifteen minutes you have a decision." The president of a $30 million family-owned chemical manufacturer in New Jersey once remarked to me that people from big companies have difficulty making quick decisions. "As much as they profess to be decision makers," he said, "they look for a decision from someone else. We don't have time for that."

Changes occur much more rapidly at small firms. "At Du Pont," said one outplaced manager, "the process from conception of an idea to realization took months. In a small company it takes weeks."

Less politics, different politics

Too much politics is a complaint more often heard at large companies. "I spent four years at Scott Paper," one small-company executive says, "and sixty percent of my time was wasted lobbying for things that I didn't know would ever happen or not. I found it very time-consuming and worthless."

"Politics" can manifest itself in other subtle ways. One CEO of a 20-person metalworking company remembers when he worked at the U.S. assembly plant of a large foreign automaker. Just when he'd finally succeeded in making his shop cost-efficient and in line with company goals, a high-ranking vice president in Europe decided to close his plant, largely to spite another vice president he was feuding with.

In a small company your personal relationship with the

president or CEO matters more than it does at a large company, where many layers may separate you from the top.

"Your relationship with your boss is very important in a small company," says a manager, who lost his job after his company merged with a rival computer manufacturer. "In a large company you don't work directly for the CEO, and you can transfer to another department if things don't work out with your immediate boss. But in a small company, once you get above a certain level and you don't tickle the CEO's fancy, you'll stagnate or be shipped out. And once they form a negative opinion of you, it's very hard to change it."

Broader responsibilities in a small company

It's not uncommon to see a collection of cowboy hats, hard hats, football helmets, baseball caps, and military caps in the president's office at a small company, as a way of symbolizing his or her versatility.

Almost every small-company executive can tell stories about visits to the warehouse to help pack boxes when a flood of orders arrives. "I might be wearing a three-piece suit in the morning, then I'll change to jeans in the afternoon and spend two hours putting parts in little plastic bags and filling out Federal Express forms. Then I'll change back into my suit and go to a dinner meeting," says one CEO.

One entrepreneur I worked with once got a rush order from a catalog company for a thousand blue Sand Sharks, a novelty item with plastic jaws that keeps beach towels anchored to the sand. It was the dead of winter, no employees were around, so the president, his partner, and their families spent a frantic weekend sorting and packaging Sand Sharks while snacking on pizza and soda pop.

At small companies job descriptions expand to fit the immediate need. At a landscaping firm in Alabama, for instance, where chain saws and high-tension wires made the free-felling work particularly dangerous, the treasurer informed the president that they needed to hire a risk manager to control their exposure to accident claims. The president quickly added "risk manager" to the treasurer's job description. As we'll mention more than once in this book, at small companies it helps to be versatile.

"You have to invent something new every day," one manager said.

Some people, of course, will find this sort of variety refreshing. Others might find it distracting. "In a small business you're bouncing around more. That can be good, but sometimes you'd rather set off in one direction and stay the course awhile," said one 57-year-old manager who had moved from a corporate job where he was "four layers away" from the actual work to a small company where he had to type his own letters.

More direct contact with the customer

Everyone at a small company is a customer-service representative. When customers call, everyone must be capable of dealing with their needs.

"Some people at large companies have never met a customer," says the CEO of a small company. A small-company manager has to find a way to be polite to a customer even when their interruptions threaten to destroy his day. "You have to be able to deal with the customer at eight A.M. when you're right in the middle of doing something else," he adds. "If you get all frustrated and bent out of shape over that kind of thing, you won't make it in a small company."

A greater need to "do more with less"

But cash flow *is* a more urgent matter at small companies than at large ones.

"What you have in some small companies," one CEO said, "is the sheer terror of knowing what is happening in your cash flow from month to month. You have people threatening you and people who owe you money, and you never know when your biggest customer might go into Chapter 11 at the same time he owes you next week's payroll. Is that better than the anxieties of working in a large, bureaucratic company? Do you sleep better at night at one or the other? I don't know."

Not every company lives on the edge, but small-company employees must know how to beg, barter, or borrow to get the resources they need. One early-stage manufacturing company, for instance, needed management training. The CEO discovered that the training department at its bank needed a refrigerator but was unable to requisition one from the bank. So the CEO offered the training department a refrigerator. In return the trainers allowed the company's managers to attend its classes.

THE ULTIMATE TRADE-OFF

Small companies, of course, go out of business with much greater frequency than large businesses do. Corporations like Johnson & Johnson, Prudential, and General Motors have been around for decades and will probably last for decades more, but you can bet that a high percentage of the high-fliers on *Inc.* Magazine's Top 100 will vanish from that list in a few years. According to *Employers Large and Small*, few start-ups survive to celebrate their fifth birthday.

But working for a large company in the 1990s has also become a gamble. To someone who has just been given notice after five, ten, or twenty years with a once-reliable employer like GM or United Technologies, working in a small company may not seem like such a risky proposition after all. As we'll repeat many times in this book, your only security is your faith in yourself and your ability to find or create your next job.

Swimming Lessons

As a job seeker your search will soon bring you to a fork in life's proverbial road. One prong of the fork—a six-lane toll road perhaps—will lead toward the towers of big business. The other fork—a meandering ribbon of two-lane blacktop, or maybe a country lane—will lead toward the Quonset huts of small business. Only you can decide which fork looks best to you.

This chapter should help you make that decision by pointing out the differences between large and small companies. Those differences, of course, consist of shades of gray rather than a simple contrast of white on black. But the differences are very real, and only when you've considered them carefully and compared them to your own temperament, talents, and goals can you decide which fork in the job-search road will lead you to your personal promised land.

Tips

- If you don't like the politics of a large company, try small-company life. But be forewarned: Just as small towns can have a busier gossip mill than big cities, small companies often have their own intense brand of politics.
- Compensation packages at small companies are more likely to be open for negotiation, with pay pegged to performance and often a chance to accrue equity in the company.
- As we'll repeat many times in this book, your only security is your faith in yourself and your ability to find or create your next job.
- "When you're growing a company," a small-company vice president once noted, "the order of the day is all-hands-on-deck. If you don't perform, there's no place to hide." Your successes and failures will be more conspicuous in a small company.
- One small-firm CEO says, "You want to know what delegation is in a small company?" He took a pencil in his right hand and transferred it to his left. "*That's* delegation in a small company."

CHAPTER THREE

The Bullfrog: Understanding the Mind of the Small-Company CEO

The CEO of a small business is like a bullfrog sitting at the edge of a rural pond. There he (or she) sits in that glass-walled corner office, like a bullfrog enthroned on a muddy bank. Both CEOs and bullfrogs rule, or so it appears, as the lords and masters of their small kingdoms. Both are capable of tremendous leaps of enthusiasm and imagination, in their own unique ways. And both seem to enjoy announcing their dominion over all they survey—or so you'd gather from listening to their authoritative croaks.

While conducting searches for small companies, I've met dozens of "bullfrogs." On the whole they are confident, imaginative, risk-taking mavericks with strong, vivid personalities. They take a defiant pride in the businesses they've built brick by brick from the ground up. If I were stranded on a desert island—or marooned at some rural pond—I'd choose these bullfrogs for company.

But to the job seeker who's unfamiliar with the small-company job market, the bullfrog may speak a language that's difficult to understand. Unlike Fortune 1000 managers, who tend to adhere to standardized hiring procedures, most small-business people have their own individualized notions about how to find and hire new employees. And the smaller the business, the more individualized the hiring process will be. The challenge for the job seeker is to customize his or her approach to the "bull-frog" by learning as much as possible about the company in advance.

TWO TYPES OF BULLFROGS: THE GROWTH JUNKIES AND THE INCOME SUBSTITUTORS

Bullfrogs can be quickly categorized into one of two types. First there are the growth junkies, who constantly hatch plans for expanding their businesses, renting new spaces, and seducing bigger customers. They're determined to grow wealthy, but money alone never satisfies them. If their business plateaus, they liquidate and start over. They often make their key employees rich, but they also drive them crazy.

Other bullfrogs simply want the good life. They strive for nothing more than a suburban home, two cars in the garage, and enough money to send their kids to college and retire to the gulf coast of Florida. They just want a quiet business to go to every day where they can work with all the peace and tranquillity of a bureaucrat. Their employees keep their sanity, but they rarely get rich.

Growth junkies

The growth-oriented bullfrogs are often real "characters." Unlike most of us, they aren't bound to a restrained level of decorum and self-censorship at the office. If they own the place, they may act that way. They can indulge their eccentricities, and many do.

One young real estate developer fits this description. By pulling on his own bootstraps, he has risen from a high school dropout to a small-time building contractor to a developer of hotels and office buildings. His first home was a tiny brick row house. By his early 30s, he owned a Georgian mansion on 36 acres of horse pasture in a wealthy suburb and was hosting fund-raisers for big-time political candidates.

He was in perpetual motion, obsessed with adding business after business to his overleveraged empire. He chain-smoked while taking high-blood-pressure medication. To be near him was to be intoxicated by the sense that vast wealth was only a venture away. "I'm going to make somebody rich today," he'd say, wrapping his arm around you.

Keeping up with his flights of fancy could be exhausting. While waiting for gifts to be wrapped at a department store, he might kill time by posing as a floorwalker, or convince a clerk that today was his wedding day, or suddenly hatch an idea for a new spa where rich smokers (like himself) could end their addiction. He often threw tantrums and threatened his foes with bodily harm. Yet he could be utterly charming if he took you into his confidence, and he called his mother every day on his car phone.

Entrepreneurs are stereotyped as being wild men. They've been compared to cars equipped with a five-speed transmission in which the first four don't work. They are fine for cruising along at 60 miles per hour, but conk out below 30 miles per hour. Entrepreneurs are great when growth is the order of the day; they don't perform as well in stable environments.

But they're often misunderstood. Most are motivated by a desire to achieve rather than to accumulate wealth. They take enormous risks, but most of them look before they leap into a major investment or venture. They're individualistic but not necessarily eccentric.

The income substitutors

The vast majority of small businesses in the United States, however, are run by people who have much more modest ambitions. Their businesses reach their final size when they open one office and employ two or three people. They are known as "income substitutors."

Income substitutors range from the proprietor of the local pizza parlor, the bed-and-breakfast, or the video-rental store to doctors or lawyers in solo practices, free-lance writers, and former executives who buy turnkey franchises and operate them with their spouses.

"Their main purpose is to establish a substitute form of income that does not entail working for someone else," writes David Birch in *Job Creation in America.* You might see a BMW or Mercedes parked outside their office. But unlike the growth junkies, they have no plans to build an empire or employ dozens of people.

The job seeker should find out what the employer's ambitions are. If you're looking for a stable environment and not a vehicle for growth, the income substitutor might be your kind of bullfrog.

THE BULLFROG'S THREE BIGGEST DESIRES

All small-company presidents tend to have at least three questions on their mind when they evaluate the people who reach the finals of a search campaign. They want to know if you will:

• *Add value* to the company, perhaps by furnishing the skills or experience that the company needs at the moment. Can you furnish one or more of the missing pieces of my puzzle?

• *Fit into the culture* of a small company, where every employee must be versatile, resourceful, and committed to the same goals.

• *Be compatible with me.* Would you complement my

strengths, stand up well under pressure, and get along with me in a close-knit working environment?

The bullfrog will have lots of more specialized questions, but when we asked small-company CEOs what they were looking for in new employees, their concerns kept falling into these three categories. Your answers to these questions will determine whether you're seriously considered for the job—and more importantly, whether you and the company are right for each other.

"Can you add value to my business?"

A bullfrog needs to know if you can fatten the bottom line, add another dimension to his or her palette of expertise, and help the company reach the level it's striving for. Usually a company has an immediate problem that can't be solved or a growth opportunity that can't be taken advantage of by anyone currently on the payroll.

If you can convince the interviewer that you can solve that problem, you'll make a very favorable impression. The door will open, just as it did for Ali Baba when he uttered the magic words in front of the cave of the Forty Thieves.

A cross-cultural negotiator needed. One CEO, for instance, needed someone who could negotiate with the foreign governments that were courting his company to build factories within their borders. The relocation would enable the $16 million company to build its high-tech computerized overhead projectors closer to its European markets. He didn't intend to advertise for such a person. But he would have hired the first person he met with experience in cross-cultural negotiation.

Combining technical with interpersonal savvy. At one computer-systems company the president is always looking for three kinds of employees. The first kind are the ones who have been in the consulting business and can bring business with them. The second are people who are familiar with the latest computer

Types of Small-Business Bullfrogs*

- *Professional Bullfrog.* This type is a veteran of a large corporation, usually hired to run a small company that has outgrown the managerial skills of the founder. Also includes leaders of spin-offs from large corporations. Usually glad to hire other corporate refugees.

- *Entrepreneur Bullfrog.* The entrepreneur is motivated more by achievement than by power or money alone. Likes to hire people who can share the dream and help make it a reality.

- *Minority Bullfrog.* This type of bullfrog—which is growing in number—is comfortable with hiring a "rainbow" work force: people of a variety of races, religions, and colors.

- *"Character" Bullfrog.* Small-business owners often indulge in nutty behavior. After all, no one can tell them not to. Before you take a job, find out what their eccentricities are and whether you can live with them.

- *Scientist Bullfrog.* Many engineers and scientists start small businesses to commercialize a breakthrough technology. They are most comfortable hiring other technical people and may seem naive about business to an experienced marketing or sales executive.

- *Income Substitutor Bullfrog.* This bullfrog owns a business that's tiny and profitable and wants to keep it exactly that way. They may offer limited opportunity to those who want high growth and high pay.

- *Parental Bullfrog.* Leaders of family businesses like to take people under their wing and help them grow. They may not allow nonfamily members to occupy senior positions, however.

- *Female Bullfrog.* Women CEOs are rarely in business just to make money; they have social, political, or artistic goals as well. As leaders they prefer to encourage employees rather than to intimidate them.

* Small-business CEOs may fall into several of the above categories. Consequently they'll manifest a blend of characteristics.

technology. The third kind are those with the people skills to do the postsale customer support that maintains customer loyalty. The ideal applicant would combine all of these skills. If you could show that you had two of them, you'd get the job on the spot. The smaller the consulting firm, the more the bullfrog needs someone with multiple skills. "One of my biggest problems," said this bullfrog, "is waiting for a twenty-eight-year-old technical whiz to develop the interpersonal savvy to work with our Fortune 100 clients."

A marketer who knows the M.D. market. In the case of the vice president of a Boston medical-products company, he wasn't entirely sure how to cheaply and effectively reach his market— endocrinologists and internists—with information about his product. Recruit a highly respected doctor and urge him to tell his colleagues? Send letters to every endocrinologist? Advertise in a medical journal? "The last thing we need is someone giving us an amateur opinion on that question, but we could really use somebody who had experience doing exactly that type of marketing," this V.P. says.

Searching for the perfect fit. Some small-company presidents only hire someone with the "perfect fit." One psychologist whose young company distributes therapeutic games to educators and child psychologists used to hire friends and acquaintances. But when his fledgling business began to lose money, he saw only three options: close the company down, maintain it as a very expensive hobby, or replace his amateur employees with professionals. He chose the third option.

He now places ads in *The New York Times, The Washington Post,* and *The Philadelphia Inquirer,* targeting people who had experience marketing children's products through the mail. After receiving hundreds of resumes, he picks the person who knows how to do exactly that. "At a certain stage you grow because your ideas are good, but then you need experience," he says. "I was looking for a perfect fit." Of his two top managers, one had worked at the Spiegel catalog and the other at Bantam Doubleday Dell.

It never hurts to ask. The point here is that the best way to show potential employers that you can add value to their business is by finding out what their most pressing problems are and then suggesting that you know how to solve them. But how do you find out what those problems are? It never hurts to ask. He or she might tell you. Also, by the time of your interview you'll have gathered a truckload of information about the company through library research and personal networking.

Until you've identified the company's most pressing needs, you can't determine whether you can make the kind of tangible contribution that small-business owners are looking for. But if you can demonstrate that your skills apply to the company's needs, you're likely to get a job, or at least a consulting assignment.

"Will you fit in at a small business?"

Small-business people, especially those who have never experienced the corporate world, need to know whether a candidate understands the small-company culture. They wonder if someone who hasn't worked in a small firm can adjust to an ever-changing climate where cash flow is tight, quick thinking is essential, and the future is not always discernible through the economic mists.

For instance, one former Fortune 500 manager committed a major faux pas when, after joining a small telemarketing company, he continued to start off his day by sipping a cup of coffee and slowly reading *The Wall Street Journal.* That was the standard behavior for managers at his old corporation. But by hanging on to his old habits, he showed that he didn't yet understand that there's no time for such luxuries in a small business. His new boss—who happened to be his wife—soon changed his ways.

Do you embrace change? One president of a company that exports electronic overhead projectors worries that people from large companies are used to following policies that change gradually if at all. He's concerned that they would be lost in an environment in which improvisation in the face of unexpected events is an almost daily requirement. "We try to hire people who are not only willing to change but who embrace change," he said. "Small growth companies aren't like family businesses that are going to stay the same for years. Growth companies either grow and change dramatically or they go out of business."

Can you sell your ideas? Another small-company manager especially values people who not only come up with good ideas but who can also express them in a compelling way. "The most important question we have for a job applicant is, 'Can you sit at our conference table and articulate a good idea in such a way that we can all see that it's a good idea?' " he says. "Are you likely to become intimidated, or angry, or defensive during a heated discussion, or can you regulate your emotional response in a way that contributes to a good working environment?"

Can you adjust to a shoestring budget? Like aristocracy whose fortunes were wiped out by war or revolution, many people who have left large companies have difficulty living within a small-company budget. One founder of a high-tech business who had hired an ex-IBM executive to manage the company soon clashed with the new manager over how much salary and how much commission to pay the company's salesmen. The former IBMer favored a higher base salary, because IBM salesmen are used to servicing stable accounts and couldn't survive on commission. But a small, growing company needs a steady stream of new accounts, and its salesmen have to work largely on commission. In this case the last straw that got the former IBM executive fired occurred when he spent $150 on a private limousine to the airport when a $12 shuttle bus would have sufficed.

Will you be compatible with me?"

Most people gravitate toward those with whom they have something in common. And in a small business the members of the team interact more closely with the president than they would in a large company. Not surprisingly, small-business people like to hire people they like and trust.

As one CEO of a market-research firm put it, "I don't hire anyone I can't have lunch with."

It's not important what you have in common. You might have a mutual friend or networking contact. You may both be computer addicts, or you may both have struggled through night school while supporting a family during the day. Both of you might have gone to the same school, or hail from the same town, or read the same books. It doesn't matter.

In one small publishing company, for instance, the editor-in-chief is partial to people who don't tower over him. (He's 5'7".) Veterans of large corporations might be more at home with other veterans of large companies. People with eclectic, zigzagging career paths might be empathetic toward a similar person. They're not necessarily looking for soul mates or clones. But if you're familiar to them, it's just one less thing both of you need to worry about.

With age, it's all relative. If you're an older worker, you're apt to find a more sympathetic reception among CEOs your age or older. If you've been pushed into early retirement by a large corporation or had your fill of corporate life, look for a president or CEO with similar experiences or notions.

In one case, a 53-year-old manager from a large chemical company was hired by a 62-year-old president of a small high-tech company who had worked years before at the same large company and had dropped out to become a big fish in his own small pond. A 57-year-old MBA who had been fired by an insurance company where he had managed 140 people was hired by a CEO in his 60s who needed someone with experience who could take over the day-to-day management of the business.

An eclectic career path can sometimes be an asset. No one likes a job hopper, but someone who has had an eclectic background and picked up a variety of skills along the way might be very appealing to some small-company bullfrogs.

One small-company executive in his mid-40s, a vice president of marketing at a fast-growing medical-products company in Boston, experimented with several careers before finding the right niche. When he needed to hire a director of reimbursement, he picked someone with a similarly eclectic background—a woman in her early 40s who'd been a nurse, a home health care specialist, an entrepreneur, a lawyer, and a consultant.

"She's a sixties kind of person," he says, like himself. "A

company like IBM would look at her resume and say, 'This person isn't serious.' But she's now doing everything we asked of her, and a bunch of things besides." In his opinion, "All interesting people have deviant career paths."

Having the right "heart." Some CEOs insist on knowing whether you will feel as passionately as they do about making their business a success. One small-company leader uses the job interview as a chance to find out.

"I sit on their side of their table [the better to read their body language], and look deep into their eyes," he says. "I tell them that people who do well here have to have the right 'heart.' They need to care. Working here is both thrilling and draining, because we're fighting every minute to survive and grow and get to the next level. When somebody doesn't work out here, it's not because of a lack of skills but because of their attitude. The rest of us would rather work 80-hour weeks and give up weekends than hire somebody who isn't great."

Where it's easy being green. When Kermit the Frog sings, "It's not easy being green," he's talking about the color of his skin. But in the business world, *green* means friendly to the earth. A growing number of so-called green businesses are looking for socially conscious people who want to make the world a better place. At Bagel Works, Inc., for instance, the wholesaler-retailer of organically prepared bagels in New England, the president has created special questionnaires to help him select job seekers who share his environmentalist and communal values.

"We look at the mind-set as much as the experience," says Richard French, one of four young entrepreneurs who started the company with SBA loans and family savings after graduating from the University of Vermont in the late 1980s. "There needs to be mutual bonding and respect."

"Here comes one of us." Some small-company CEOs got their education in the school of hard knocks and feel a natural affinity for others who did the same. The president of one Detroit tool-and-die maker, a self-made millionaire of Polish extraction, started out as an elementary school teacher. He sold auto parts on the side and saved enough money to buy an eight-person machine shop. Then he spent 25 years carving out a niche in the cutthroat world of supplying the Big Three automakers. He likes to hire people who earned their degrees at night while working during the day—just as he did.

Some employers just naturally identify with the underdog. Take Robert C., president of a small company that grew canta-loupes and other fruits in the Dominican Republic for import to the northeastern United States during the winter. On his visits to farms in the Caribbean he would walk down the rows of cantaloupes and greet the field hands by name. "When people saw me coming," he says with pride, "they didn't say, 'Here comes the boss.' They said, 'Here comes one of us.' "

Mr. C. was the product of an Italian-Slovakian family who had earned an MBA at night and became a turnaround specialist for financially troubled small businesses. Although he couldn't pay his Dominican laborers more than $3 a day, he often brought them gifts of athletic shoes and other American goods during his visits.

The minority bullfrog. Minority employers have the same needs and concerns as other small-company CEOs. Often they're glad to hire and promote members of the same minority. But minority CEOs may decide to hire other minorities simply because they feel more comfortable working with a heterogeneous mix of people. On the other hand, competence is still the most important criterion.

"I believe that because God gave me the intelligence to be in business for myself, I should try to help members of minority groups," says a 32-year-old African-American MBA who founded a fast-growing computer-services company.

"I hire all kinds of people, but I will try to find a minority person first if I can. If I have a developmental slot, I will definitely look for a black person," he adds. Whomever he hires, however, still has to please the marketplace.

But minority bullfrogs face the same type of pressures that all bullfrogs face when they hire new employees. One black vice president said that he worries about hiring and promoting too many other black workers for fear of being accused of discrimination against whites. The truth about minority bullfrogs is that they have the same goals, methods, and anxieties as other employers.

Better to complement the CEO than be a clone. On the other hand, many small-company executives have been burned by the mistake of hiring a "clone" of themselves rather than someone with more relevant experience. One of my clients, the young president of a small manufacturing company, hired me to help him search for a veteran manager with big-company experience who could help professionalize his plant in a way that he—a person with a technical rather than a managerial background— could not.

After interviewing several senior managers, he decided to hire someone like himself—a young technology junkie with underdeveloped people skills. He soon alienated the rest of the staff and was fired. This case was, in a sense, the exception that proves the rule: It demonstrates just how difficult it can be for small-business people to hire someone who comes from outside their sphere of familiarity.

Warts and all. Does all this mean that you can't get a job if you don't have anything in common with the executive who hires you? Not necessarily. It only means that it's important to try to establish common ground. And take heart: Whatever warts you think you may have, there lives a bullfrog who has the same warts and thinks yours are quite attractive.

Keep in mind that small-company executives can't always exactly articulate what they want. "Defining the ideal job candidate is like trying to define pornography," says one CEO. "I'll know it when I see it." Their companies may be growing so fast that they don't know whom to hire first. "Whatever you want to do, I probably need two of you," one managing director says.

If they dawdle over a decision, it may be because they can't afford to hire the wrong person. "The single most expensive cost to a small business is a hiring mistake," a small-firm president says. And it's an expense that comes right out of the bullfrog's own pocket, not out of a corporate budget.

Swimming Lessons

This chapter, I hope, will provide a sense of what might be going through the small-company CEO's mind when he or she interviews job candidates. By understanding the bullfrog's concerns, you'll be better able to anticipate the sorts of questions that might arise during the interview.

At the same time the information in this chapter should remind you that, like small companies themselves, every small-company employer is unique. They range from the conservative to the flamboyant, from the sympathetic to the imperious. Understanding the range of personalities that the bullfrog might possess will help you identify the one with whom you'd be most compatible.

Since you're more likely in a small firm to have daily contact with the CEO or president, your mutual chemistry will determine how happy and successful you'll be in your job—which will determine how happy you'll be in general. In short, never take a job at a small company without thoroughly assessing the personality of the bullfrog and your compatibility with him or her.

Tips

🐸 When you work for entrepreneurs, remember that they're paying you out of their own pockets and will judge you by how good an investment you are. In big companies the money comes from a large and impersonal source; not so in a small company.

🐸 To thrive in a small company, you must be compatible with the owner or president. Any friction within the management team will be amplified by the intimate working conditions of a small company.

🐸 Dispense with bull when talking to a bullfrog: don't second-guess what they're thinking about, just figure out the clearest and most positive way to present yourself.

🐸 The best entrepreneurs are motivated by a desire to achieve, as

well as to accumulate wealth. They take enormous risks, but
they're not reckless.
ペ To understand the bullfrog, recognize that they make little
distinction between their professional and their personal lives.
Your relationship with them could be both professional and
personal.
ペ Small-business CEOs have missionary zeal. You have to share
their passion without being overwhelmed by their strong
personalities.

CHAPTER FOUR

The Female of the Species:
The Lady Bullfrog

Bullfrogs, strictly speaking, are not always men. And neither are all business owners.

In fact, during the 1980s, women formed small businesses at twice the rate of men. And in 1993 America's 5 million or so women-owned businesses employed 11 million people—the same number employed by the Fortune 500. By the year 2000, women will own nearly half of all small businesses in the United States, according to the Small Business Administration.

Women start their own businesses for the same reasons men do: for independence and self-expression. Most recently, frustration with the corporate "glass ceiling" has also spurred business ownership among women. With talented female managers far outnumbering the vacancies open to them in the upper tiers of large companies, women are choosing to become CEOs and presidents by digging "ponds" of their own.

Armed with law, accounting, medical, and engineering degrees in record numbers, women are starting or managing a wide range of small businesses, including accounting firms, publishing companies, advertising agencies, health care practices, and manufacturing and construction firms. Women entrepreneurs aren't limiting themselves to traditional service and retail businesses.

The effects of this trend have begun to be documented. Surveys show that women employers exhibit different managerial styles than men, offer more opportunities to workers of all races, genders, and colors, and place as much value on social and personal ethics as they do on making money.

Women's role in the small-business economy is still relatively small—their businesses are, on average, slightly smaller, stabler, and less growth-oriented than men's small businesses. But that's changing, and the odds that any one of us will work for a woman-owned small business at some point in our careers are increasing every day. For that reason alone this trend deserves exploration.

A BUMPER CROP OF FEMALE BULLFROGS

In 1990 an estimated 5.4 million women owned businesses of all sizes in the United States, according to the National Foundation for Women Business Owners. That represented a gain of 57 percent since 1982. Over 40 percent of those businesses have been in operation for at least a dozen years. Female ownership is strongly represented in fields that are growing—such as business and professional services—and only lightly represented in manufacturing and other declining sectors of the economy. It's estimated that women now own about 28 percent of all businesses in the United States, up from only 9.5 percent in 1984.

During the 1980s, says the SBA's Office of Women's Business Ownership, women started businesses at twice the rate of men, and the dollar value of their businesses soared from $98 billion in 1982 to $287 billion in 1987. Women-owned businesses are also growing in diversity: receipts of women-owned businesses in nontraditional fields such as manufacturing showed a sixfold increase between 1982 and 1987.

The percentage of women in the work force, of course, has been rising for more than 30 years. In 1960, fewer than 40 percent of American women worked outside the home. By the year 2000, 61 percent of American women will be working, and they'll comprise 47 percent of the labor force.

WHY WOMEN ARE CREATING THEIR OWN PONDS

Women start companies for the same reason men do: to be a bigger fish in a small pond. At least four possible factors are driving this trend: (a) the number of women with professional training and managerial experience is up; (b) the "glass ceiling" has prevented those women from becoming presidents of large companies; (c) many women find corporate life personally unfulfilling; and (d) business ownership gives a woman the flexibility she needs to maintain a career and raise a family. In addition, the creation of new professional organizations and loan programs that serve the female-owned business market are also furnishing women with the skills and funds they need to start businesses.

Choosing to bypass the glass ceiling

The glass ceiling—that colorless, odorless, semipermeable membrane that has long prevented women and members of ethnic or racial minorities from reaching the largely white and male-dominated upper echelons of U.S. business—still exists. Although women now account for half of the U.S. work force, they still occupy less than 5 percent of all top executive positions, according to the U.S. Department of Labor.

"Many of the people who are escaping from large companies

and starting their own businesses are women who've hit the glass ceiling and seen limited opportunities ahead of them," says Catherine White Berheide, Ph.D., a sociologist at Skidmore College and author of *Work, Family and Policy: A Global Perspective* (SUNY Press, 1994). "They see subtle but real barriers ahead and that leads them to choose to leave the company—but it's not purely by choice."

"Today there are a lot of highly educated women who have twenty-plus years of experience, who have supervised people, and are ready to take the reins—but they're still not getting the top jobs," says Rebecca Maddox, president of Capital Rose, Inc., a new firm that helps women grow their own companies.

Flexibility to have a career and a family

Self-employment can give a woman more control over her time, so that she can balance the demands of family and career. In large companies women often have to choose between the mommy track and the career track. Statistics show, for instance, that a woman's chance of becoming vice president shrinks drastically if she also happens to be a parent: more than half of all female executives at the level of vice president or higher are childless, compared with only 7 percent of all male executives.

Corporate life has lost some of its glamour

At the same time the career track is losing some of its allure for many baby-boom-generation women (and for baby-boom men as well, it might be said). "We've lived through forty years of a great experiment in corporate America, the era of the 'organization man,' " says Maddox. "That's long enough for some people to say, 'I don't like this anymore.' I remember riding the train home from New York with all the commuters. I'd look at the gray faces of the men and see the toll that corporate life had taken on them. Now people are saying, 'I need to feel good about something in my life besides this job.' "

A growing number of female professionals

Between 1983 and 1990 alone, the U.S. labor force gained 303,000 female accountants and auditors, 132,000 computer systems analysts and scientists, 80,000 financial managers, 56,000 lawyers, 29,000 physicians, and 24,000 electrical and electronic engineers. As American businesses large and small grope with a shortage of highly skilled labor in coming decades, trained women will become more valuable and more sought-after than ever.

The increasing recognition of the women's business market

Women have started to earn more respect from lenders, some of whom are beginning to recognize that female-owned businesses represent a growing market for financial services. Capital Rose, Inc., for example, was started by Ms. Maddox in Philadelphia in 1993 specifically to introduce investors, bankers, and consultants to women entrepreneurs who needed financing or advice for their businesses. The Small Business Administration also continues to operate an Office of Women's Business Ownership that helps women start businesses. Magazines such as *Entrepreneurial Woman* and *Executive Female* indicate that advertisers see women entrepreneurs as a growing market.

WOMEN MANAGERS MANAGE DIFFERENTLY

There's an old saying that you can catch more flies with honey than you can with vinegar, and that seems to be the key to the difference between male and female management styles, says Judy B. Rosener, a faculty member at the University of California, Irvine Graduate School of Management, in the *Harvard Business Review* (Nov.–Dec. 1990).

Women, she argues in an article titled "Ways Women Lead," are more likely to use a more democratic management style, often eliciting suggestions from others, working toward consensus, and using their charisma and interpersonal skills to achieve their ends. Male leaders, by contrast, have a more authoritarian style.

Women are more likely to welcome co-workers into the decision-making process and to make their subordinates feel like equals. Women also tend to shun special perks—such as reserved parking spaces or special dining rooms—that set them apart from employees of lower rank.

This style of leadership, says Rosener, comes naturally to women, who have traditionally played the role of the nurturer in Western society. Women are now finding that the same interpersonal skills that equipped them to be good mothers, teachers, and nurses also prepare them to be effective managers—perhaps even more effective than men.

But what about the notorious overaggressive "queen bee" types that are sometimes found in large organizations, you might ask. Some experts believe that women, paradoxically, practice a softer style when they're in charge than they do when they are middle managers in big corporations. Why? Because they feel more secure in their power. "When a woman has her own business, she can be who she really is," agrees Maddox. "She doesn't have to fit into a mold. Outside of the large corporation women will put a greater emphasis on relationships. They will be more likely to give constructive feedback so that an employee can grow as a person."

SMALL BUSINESS OFFERS THE FREEDOM TO BE "A WHOLE PERSON"

A small company may be more sensitive to an employee's needs simply because it is less regimented, regardless of the owner's gender.

A single parent who is also a manager once told me, "When I worked for a large company, I didn't keep framed photographs of my son and daughter on the desk. Most of the male executives displayed pictures of their families on their desks or shelves, but I felt inhibited about it. I didn't talk about my children either. As a woman I had to avoid giving the impression that my family might be more important to me than my career, or that I was a 'traditional' mother.

"But when I left to work at an eighty-person company where I was one of seven senior managers, I could talk about my children with my boss and not arouse any suspicions about my loyalties and values. He even encouraged me to take time off to watch my daughter's field-hockey matches. I never had to hide the fact that I cared at least as much about my family as I did about my job."

Women's Businesses, Though Smaller, Have "a Sustaining Passion"

Traditionally banks have not been eager to loan money to women to start businesses. The reason is not that women are poor credit risks—statistics show that they are actually *less* likely to default on their loans than men are—but because they only borrow in small amounts. As one woman put it, bankers become successful by loaning $30 million, not $30,000.

Consequently you don't find a lot of women who are financing big expansions of their businesses. Thus female-owned businesses have remained relatively small. Family responsibilities also diminish the amount of time a woman might otherwise spend growing her business. But women's businesses are also more stable than male-owned businesses. Women rarely overleverage themselves, and they're usually strongly committed to what they're doing. Therefore they're less likely to fold their tents at the first economic downturn. "In women-owned businesses you often find a sustaining passion," says Maddox.

You'll Rarely Hear a Woman Say, "She Who Dies with the Most Toys Wins"

Although women entrepreneurs want to make money, they're equally motivated by nonfinancial rewards.

"Very few women say they go into business because they want to make a lot of money and drive a big Mercedes," says Maddox. "Women want to make money. But it's not unusual to hear a woman say that she's starting a business because it will be good for her, or for her kids, or for society. Women are compelled by a combination of doing good and making money. In that sense the difference between men and women is striking."

PORTRAIT OF A FEMALE ENTREPRENEUR OF THE '90s

Meet Lisa Conte. As the thirty-something founder of a Santa Clara, CA–based drug company that's as dedicated to saving the world's rain forests as it is to earning a billion dollars, she typifies the new breed of female bullfrog.

The daughter of two Long Island, NY, pharmacists, and the holder of an MBA and a master's in pharmacology, Ms. Conte happened to be reading about the vanishing rain forests a few years ago. She was struck by the news that if the rain forests disappear, thousands of natural pharmacological plants, many of them currently used by native healers, or shamans, might vanish too.

Hearing the rasping knock of opportunity, she quit her job at a venture-capital firm, raised $40,000 in credit card credit, and started Shaman Pharmaceuticals, Inc. Within three years she'd raised $4 million more in venture capital, lured several talented researchers away from big pharmaceutical companies, and hired a celebrated botanist from the New York Botanical Garden to comb the jungles of Latin America and Africa for healing plants that might be used as the basis for new mass-market medications.

As of January 1993, Shaman Pharmaceuticals had already formed a marketing and manufacturing partnership with an Italian drug company, was pursuing FDA approval of its first antiviral product, and was preparing for an initial public offering.

With her professional degrees and ability to raise large amounts of capital, Ms. Conte has some of the same entrepreneurial advantages that men have traditionally had. She represents a new generation of women who have achieved the same level of schooling and training as their male contemporaries. Consequently they are beginning to break into the kind of lucrative fields that men have long monopolized.

THE "GIRLS" NOW HAVE THEIR OWN "OLD-GIRL NETWORK"

In fact so many women have entered the business world that an "old-girl network" has begun to rival the traditional "old-boy network." Take, for example, a young accountant, Patricia M., who became a big fish at a small pond by moving from a mid-level position in a "Big Six" accounting firm to a controller's job at one of the small companies she'd been assigned to audit. During her visits to the company she befriended a female vice president, who helped her get the job.

At the Big Six firm Ms. M. had contended with a male-dominated atmosphere in which women were almost but not quite equal. The female accountants believed they were assigned to audit smaller companies than the men. Nor were the women included in many of the men's ritual sports outings.

This vague bias against her gender didn't affect her much until she became pregnant. In theory the firm offered young mothers the opportunity to work part-time. But in practice it required part-timers to produce the same amount of work as full-timers and demanded that they work full-time during the hectic quarterly reporting periods. The high-pressure world of accounting just doesn't accommodate working mothers very well.

"Accounting is still very male dominated," she says with a shrug. "At least half of the new hires are women, but there are still very few women at the manager or partner level, and the firm makes it almost impossible for them to continue if they have a child." Of two women partners, she pointed out, one has no children and the other has chosen to hire a live-in nanny.

Playing field more level in small business

So when the baby was born, she quit her job. Six months later, however, she heard from a woman who was the controller at a small investment-adviser firm she'd audited for five consecutive years. She was invited to work part-time, and that led to a full-time controller's job when her mentor moved on. "The woman who hired me had a daughter and knew what it was like to have a child and work at the same time. In this company there's still an old-boy network, and there are only two women and eighteen men among the money managers. But the playing field is a lot more level."

Now she has the kind of smorgasbord of responsibilities that she didn't have at the larger firm. No longer merely an auditor, she hires her own assistants, writes the company personnel-policy manual, manages the payroll taxes, and does the actual number crunching that most controllers at larger companies would automatically delegate to a junior accountant. "I have to push a pencil. A lot of people from big companies won't do that. But I love it. I like being the only one in my department. I'm not living under a huge structure that was set up years ago and will never change. On the whole I'm better off."

WOMEN ARE LEADING TRADITIONALLY MALE-DOMINATED BUSINESSES

Female bullfrogs can be found in every industry. Take, for instance, Aleda Loughman, president and COO of Somat Corp., a $7.5 million, 50-employee company in southeastern Pennsylvania. Somat's principal product is a sophisticated trash compactor that mixes refuse and garbage with water, compresses the mixture, the separates the water from the waste and recycles the water back to the compactor. Cruise ships, for example, use them to compress their trash and economize on fresh water. She joined the company in 1957 as the founder's secretary. A single mother with a high school diploma, she gradually assumed marketing, sales, personnel, and financial duties before becoming vice president in 1976. In 1986, after she trained four successive male CEOs who tried and failed to lead the company adequately, she assumed the top job at the board of directors' request.

She is hardly the only woman to run a business in a

traditionally male industry. Members of the National Association of Women Business Owners include the presidents of a plastics-molding company, an environmental construction firm, and a floor-covering installation company.

Optimal Candidate: You don't have to be a woman to work at a female-owned or operated business. But you do need to be able to accept women as authority figures. Men who have worked in male-dominated corporations where they have had little experience working with women other than subordinates may have to do some soul-searching before they take a job at a female-owned company.

In general, women leaders create a more cooperative, less hierarchical culture where information is shared rather than hoarded and people are valued as much as profits are. Other women, members of minority groups, older workers, and those who want to integrate their personal and professional lives might find enjoyable work in a female-owned business. Parents of small children or adults caring for elderly parents might find that women small-business owners are more sensitive to their needs for flexible working hours and other benefits.

But I don't want to overstate the case: women business owners, in many ways, are just as interested in achieving success as men are. The gender of the employer is only one of several factors—along with stage of development, form of ownership, industry, and so forth—that determine the company's needs and culture.

Swimming Lessons

The number of female-owned businesses in the United States is growing rapidly. Women now own more than a fourth of all businesses in the country, and during the 1980s the value of their businesses tripled to almost $300 billion.

Women business owners differ from male business owners in management style and in the type of corporate culture they create. Women are more likely to be as concerned with people as they are with profits, and more interested in achieving stability than producing rapid growth.

This chapter should help you decide whether or not you'd like to work for a woman. If so, you can locate women-owned businesses by contacting the nearest chapter of the National Association of Women Business Owners, by seeking out organizations such as Capital Rose, Inc., and by pursuing your contacts within the female small-business community (see the chapter on networking in Part Two of this book.)

The days when women merely owned beauty parlors and gift shops are coming to an end. Women today run accounting firms, advertising agencies, and even factories. As bankers become more willing to lend money to women, as high-quality day care becomes more available, and as the old-boy network becomes less powerful, women will become more prominent in business, and the chances will become even greater that at some point in our careers we'll be working for a female of the species.

Tips

❊ Don't ignore women-owned businesses. America's five million or so women-owned businesses currently employ 11 million people—the same number employed by the Fortune 500. By the year 2000, women will own nearly half of all small businesses in the United States.

❊ Female managers welcome people into the decision-making process and are more likely to make their subordinates feel like equals. Women also tend to shun special perks that set them apart from employees of lower rank.

❊ Tap into your local and national women's network. Some areas have Yellow Pages devoted entirely to women-owned enterprises. Look for the nearest chapter of the National Association of Women Business Owners.

CHAPTER FIVE

Dissecting the Bullfrog:
How to Understand the Various
Types of Small-Business Employers

As part of the research for this book I created focus groups in which a total of 21 successful CEOs and presidents were asked to gather in banquet rooms at a suburban hotel and share their philosophies about evaluating job candidates and hiring new employees.

The criteria for being invited was that the guest be the founder, president, or CEO of a small, thriving company. The companies and CEOs we chose represented a cross-section of the small-business world. They came from a wide variety of industries, stages, and forms of ownership.

We divided them into three groups. The first group included six people who started businesses in cellular-telephone networks, prerecorded disk-jockey tapes, hospital construction, and neighborhood banking. The second group was composed of eight people whose companies produced goods such as candy, medical devices, silver kaleidoscopes, and computer peripherals. The third group included the presidents of seven professional services companies—such as accounting, information systems, and market research—to large companies.

How Three Kinds of Bullfrogs Hire

For several hours these "bullfrogs" discussed the methods they use to find new employees, interview and screen them, and respond to resumes and cover letters, in addition to personality traits they look for. Their comments and advice can be found peppered throughout this book.

But the focus groups yielded another, unexpected dividend. It was clear that each group had its own distinctive tone and character. Members of the first group, whom I'll call Prometheans, were all involved in very early-stage companies. They were expressive and passionate. They wore their emotions on their sleeves. Members of the second group, which was made up primarily of manufacturing-firm presidents, were direct and opinionated, for the most part. The members of the third group, all of whom were consultants who provided accounting, marketing, and other services to large companies, were the most intellectual, and the most difficult to read.

The focus-group results suggested to us that a job seeker can to some extent predict the temperament and expectations of a "bullfrog" by finding out whether he or she is a Promethean, a manufacturer, or a provider of professional services, as we've chosen to label them. If you can tell one type from the other, you'll have one more tool for discovering whether you and your prospective employer would hit it off.

The Prometheans

The mythical Prometheus, the Titan who stole fire from the gods and gave it to mortals, has come to symbolize creativity and courageous originality. That's why I call the first group Prometheans. They're the people who start companies from scratch.

Among them was an African-American woman who'd left Wall Street to produce CD-ROM disks for children; a man who started a cellular-phone company after his small chain of retail appliance stores went under; a woman who started her own construction-management firm; a man in his 30s who'd built a lucrative disk-jockey booking agency; and a young lawyer who started a computer-training service.

Prometheans like people young and hungry. Prometheans located most of their new employees through networking. They favor young people because they're loyal, eager to learn, and don't require a great deal of money.

"My big concern with someone new," said one entrepreneur, who said she quit investment banking because it had no soul, "is, will I like you, will I respect you, will I like working with you? I'm looking for colleagues, not people to supervise."

Outplaced executives who've worked for one company for 10 or 20 years and are accustomed to lots of staff support and regular pay increases might not be compatible with a Promethean, who can't promise either of those things.

"One plus one must equal three." Most of all, Prometheans look for high productivity. "When will you pay for yourself?" was one entrepreneur's unspoken question for job candidates. Another said, "One plus one has to equal three. I have to be convinced that I'll be better off if they're working for me."

One entrepreneur wants to know right away if a job candidate is a doer or if he is "shrubbery." "That's what I call people who just stand at the cash register or sit at a desk," he says.

When the time came to adjourn, members of the other two groups dispersed quickly, but the Prometheans lingered. They networked. They discussed potential partnerships. When it comes to hatching deals, Prometheans can't seem to help themselves.

The Manufacturers

The second focus group consisted of eight presidents and CEOs of manufacturing firms ranging in size from 20 employees to 500 employees. One was a teacher who had turned her hobby of making silver kaleidoscopes into a business. Another had helped her father manufacture plastic notebinders since college. There was a former Pratt & Whitney engineer who rose to president of an integrated-circuit manufacture, the owner of a fourth-generation family candy manufacturer, and a chemist who'd started a biotech company. With the exception of the kaleidoscope maker, the manufacturers hadn't started their businesses.

High-tech versus low-tech manufacturers. In temperament and approach to hiring, this group broke down into two subgroups. In one subgroup the members were sophisticated Ph.D.s and MBAs with large-company experience who had been hired to run small high-tech corporations. They tended to be competitive, impatient, and confrontational. When hiring new people, they use the same testing and recruiting tools that large companies use. They don't hire on gut instincts.

The second subgroup of manufacturers came from noncorporate backgrounds and ran family or founder-based businesses. One, the owner of a family candy business, had a hiring style that could best be described as taking people under his wing. Ordinarily he hires only people he's known for at least a year.

No gimmicky resumes. Manufacturers didn't like "gimmicky" or overly "creative" resumes. Most of all, they like to see aggressiveness in a job candidate. "It's all about hustle," said one. "If you send a resume, call and follow it up. Show initiative. You can't follow up too much. The worst that will happen is that you won't get the job. But you definitely won't get the job if you're not aggressive."

The bullfrog's background makes all the difference. Bullfrogs at small manufacturing companies vary widely in personality and style. If they came to small companies after working for large corporations, they'll exhibit a polished, somewhat standardized, style. If they have always worked in small business, they may create a familial culture within their companies.

Professional Service Providers

Seven presidents or owners of consulting firms that provide professional services such as accounting, market research, computer systems, public relations, and financial services made up the third focus group. They were complex, brainy people who have technical expertise and a flair for pleasing customers. They prefer to hire people with the same combination of skills.

They'll look at you through their clients' eyes. This kind of employer will study you very closely during an interview. "We ask each applicant to make a presentation to a group in our company. We try to see them through a client's eyes," said one owner. "I try to envision the person in a social setting with me and my best friends," said another. A third said that he watched to see how a male candidate shook a woman's hand: "A man who won't shake a woman's hand properly probably feels threatened by her."

Presidents of marketing and advertising firms naturally respond to creative salesmanship from a job applicant (such as sending a cake inscribed with the applicant's name, as mentioned in Chapter Thirteen) more readily than the president of a small accounting firm or law firm will. Advertising and marketing executives will often judge you by how creatively you market or advertise yourself to them.

They prefer candidates who project a professional image. During an interview they try to find out whether the candidate could improvise a conversation and do more than just volley questions and answers back and forth. They hire people who can convert awkward silences into laughter. Like veteran poker players, they may remain stone-faced, watching you for clues to your talents, motivations, and flaws. Ultimately they will hire people who have the right blend of technical expertise and interpersonal skills.

Each member of this group, I should point out, had spent several years working in a large corporation. Then they went out on their own and began selling services to large companies by using their old contacts. If you've come from a large company, but needed more excitement and creativity, you might be very comfortable with them.

Swimming Lessons

My focus groups taught me that small-company presidents often fall into one of the three discernible categories: The Prometheans, the manufacturers, and the professional service providers. You can predict a lot about the behavior of a business owner or CEO if you can find out which group he or she belongs to.

The Prometheans love taking risks and watching businesses grow. When they've achieved success, they often get bored and decide to sell the business and start all over. The manufacturers are an opinionated, macho crowd, far more interested in gadgets than emotions. The consultants are perhaps the least readable and most intriguing of the three types: they use a combination of brains and charm to win and hang on to their wealthy, demanding, and sometimes temperamental clients.

If you're young, energetic, and don't need a lot of security or cash, you might be perfect for a firm run by a pure entrepreneur. If you have a $2,000-a-month mortgage, two kids in college, and an ailing parent, you won't look attractive to an entrepreneur. If you're an electronics buff who would rather discuss computers at a cocktail party than talk about people, you'll probably be comfortable in an interview with a manufacturer. But if you're a bubbly marketing type, manufacturers may not have an immediate rapport with you. If you're equally at home with technology and people, can think both logically and intuitively, and can blend professional skills with polished salesmanship, you might be right for a high-tech consulting firm.

Owners or presidents of small businesses, of course, do not fit neatly into the easily identifiable molds. They do not have entirely predictable temperaments or tastes. On the contrary, when approaching the small-business person, take nothing for granted. But there are "types," and you'll be better prepared to deal with the bullfrog if you know whether he (or she) is a Promethean, a manufacturer, or a professional services provider.

Keep in mind, too, that you've got to understand yourself before you can determine which kind of employer or industry suits you best. You must assess your skills, your abilities, and your preferences. (See Chapter Seven for a description of how I arrived at an understanding of my needs and wants, and how you might do the same.)

Tips

❧ Entrepreneurs, especially when first starting a business, like to hire young, energetic, unmarried people who will gladly work long hours at relatively low pay in return for a chance to prove themselves.

❧ Manufacturers respond best to aggressive job candidates with strong credentials who don't try to impress them with cute cover letters or gimmicky resumes.

❧ Professional service providers are a complex, intellectual breed. They need highly educated people with advanced technical expertise who also have sophisticated interpersonal skills. They'll look at you through their clients' eyes, so approach them as though you were calling on an important client.

CHAPTER SIX

What Small-Company Managers Really Do

Job titles do not always signify the same things in small companies that they do in large ones. Job seekers often see newspaper ads for specific openings in small firms and assume that those jobs entail the same routines they were accustomed to in a large company.

But, as the lyricist Ira Gershwin wrote, "It ain't necessarily so."

For instance, a large-company controller's principal responsibility might be to relay the policies handed down by the executive committee to the chief financial officers at each subsidiary and ensure their execution. In a large company that chore alone might consume half the week.

But the same controller, arriving at a small company, might

be held responsible for a bottomless grab bag of duties. He might have to teach himself new spreadsheet programs, juggle accounts receivable and payable, answer the phone during the receptionist's lunch break, hire a bookkeeper and a junior accountant, and drop everything when the outside auditors make their annual rounds.

In other words small-company managers must cheerfully handle many of the tasks that their counterparts in large companies would ordinarily delegate to their underlings. Instead of sitting on top of an organizational pyramid, the small-company manager may be the entire pyramid.

If you don't mind switching back and forth among a wide variety of tasks during the day, you might like working in a small company. "I'm lucky. That kind of thing doesn't get me flustered," said the office manager of a five-person computer-reselling company. Other people go crazy if distractions keep derailing their train of thought.

By the same token, you must be a hands-on type of manager to like working in a small company. Many corporate job seekers like to think of themselves as "hands-on," but I've often witnessed the shock suffered by people from large companies when they transfer to small companies and have to learn how to use a word processor and type their own letters for the first time.

On the following pages I've illustrated the differences between job responsibilities for people with the same title at large and small companies. If the small-company job description sounds attractive, you might do swimmingly in a small pond.

PRESIDENT

The president of a company is a company's ultimate decision maker, unless he or she is overshadowed by a powerful chairman or board of directors. At a large company the president plays a role analogous to that of the president of the United States. He or she represents the company to the outside world, makes decisions based on the information supplied by the top advisers, and remains fairly distant from the shop floor where the actual work is done.

At a small company the president is involved in every aspect of the business, from strategic planning to equipment repair. He or she will probably be the company's top salesperson, its chief equipment repairer, and its director of human resources. More importantly he or she is the company's lender of last resort, often dipping into personal savings or mortgaging his home in order to obtain loans and meet payroll.

Duties of the president of a <u>large</u> company:

• Develops and maintains a positive company image and positive relations between the company, key customers, vendors, and regulators.

• Serves as the final authority for employee relations. Holds ultimate authority over hiring and firing decisions, union negotiations, and the administration of formal disciplinary actions.

• Directs the activities of the vice presidents of finance, manufacturing, marketing, sales, human resources, and information services.

• Develops plans for the growth and development of the company and the expansion or improvement of the physical plant, usually with the assistance of the vice presidents of finance and administration and the general manager.

• Ensures that company operations comply with all applicable laws and regulations.

• Handles all negotiations with outside parties on behalf of the company.

Duties of the president of a <u>small</u> company:

• Invents the product. Develops the products on which the company is predicated.

- Raids savings and takes out a second mortgage to raise financing if necessary.
- Buys, puts together, and figures out how to operate new equipment, and teaches new employees how to use it.
- Sells, sells, sells as if the company's life depended upon it—which it does.
- Staffs the company with former colleagues, friends, and relatives, including parents, children, aunts, uncles, and siblings.
- Writes and rewrites business plans and cash-flow projections on a personal computer, usually after normal business hours. Replaces ink cartridge for the computer, refills the photocopier with toner and paper, and performs minor repairs on the copier.
- Tirelessly assures others of the company's brilliant future.
- Creates personnel policies on the fly.
- Goes to the library to research regulatory issues rather than call a lawyer.
- Develops, along with other managers and employees, plans for the growth of the company and/or its physical plant.
- Is the last to get paid, and makes up cash-flow shortages with personal funds.
- Hounds nonpaying customers and keeps creditors at bay.

Director of Marketing and Sales

At a large company the head of the marketing department creates plans and policies that people lower in the hierarchy will implement. While he or she is ultimately responsible for meeting sales goals, most of the hands-on duties—talking to customers, developing ideas for promotional campaigns—are carried out by others.

In a small company all of the marketing and sales tasks, from long-range planning to sketching out ideas for newspaper ads, might be telescoped into one enormous job. The person in that job has to be part-workhorse and part-magician, able to work evenings and produce major promotional campaigns on a minimal budget.

Duties of the director of marketing and sales at a *large* company:

- Develops and implements a marketing and sales strategy for company products, including pricing policies and packaging and advertising policies, in conjunction with the policy committee.
- Carries out a program of market research, product development, and testing, under the direction of the general manager.
- Develops a plan and support procedure for customer contracts and client services; supervises a staff of salespeople and customer-relations representatives who implement the plan.
- Advises the general manager on improving product design, distribution policies, and procedures.
- Develops and maintains relationships with advertising agencies, public relations firms, and market-research firms.

Duties of the director of marketing and sales at a *small* company:

- Meets sales quota by any means necessary—promises whatever it takes.
- Creates own sales literature, and finds a printer who'll produce it for next to nothing.
- Borrows home power saw to build trade-show booth; staffs booth at the show.
- Invents pricing, customer service, packaging, and advertising policies.
- Borrows market research from a friend at a big company.
- Persuades receptionists to double as customer-service representatives.
- Tells anyone who will listen ideas for improving product designs, distribution policies, and procedures.

- Charms ad agencies and public relations firms into donating their services.
- Creates a budget and spends only 50 percent of it, while reaching 120 percent of goal.
- Obtains mailing lists, creates mailing literature, learns how to do bulk mailings, sends out the mailing, and makes the follow-up telemarketing calls.

MANAGER OF FINANCE AND ADMINISTRATION

At a large company the chief financial officer creates policies and makes sure that the financial managers at each division comply with them. He or she meets with the company's bankers and top accountants, keeps the president aware of cash-flow problems, and stays abreast of changes in tax laws that might affect the company.

In a small company the chief financial person will be involved in all of the hands-on financial work. He or she will personally run the spreadsheets on the computer, crunch the numbers, haggle with vendors, stave off creditors, and ride herd on most purchasing decisions, whether it involves new light bulbs or a new computer system.

Duties of a manager of finance and administration at a *large* company:

- Oversees and manages all financial and office-support activities.
- Approves all agreements concerning financial obligations, such as contracts for products or services and other actions requiring a commitment of financial resources.
- Manages the cash-flow position of the company, establishes credit and collections and purchasing policies, as well as schedules for the payment of bills and other financial obligations.

- Develops and maintains relationships with financial institutions in conjunction with the president.
- Ensures the maintenance of appropriate financial records and the preparation of required financial reports.

Duties of a manager of finance and administration at a *small* company:

- Oversees and manages all financial and office-support activities; keeps the books, purchases a payroll service, manages the receptionist and bookkeeper. Hires and manages a part-time accountant.
- Devotes all available hours to auditors during the auditing period, without falling far behind on other duties.
- Responsible for negotiating lower prices on contracts than the ones agreed to.
- Purchases office furniture, indoor plants, coffee, and soft drinks.
- Provides financial counseling to the president when accompanying him or her on "dog-and-pony shows" intended to gain additional funding.
- Recommends solutions when shortfalls make it impossible to meet payroll.
- Tries to figure out what kind of computer system to buy.
- Explains to vendors why they won't be paid on time.
- Works weekends to pack crates and boxes during Christmas and other rush periods.
- Fields customer and employee complaints and solves them before they reach the president.
- Worries about insurance liability and tries to establish a safety policy.

PRODUCTION MANAGER

The head of production in a large company acts as a middleman between top management and the factory floor. His or her principal chore is to make sure that standards, deadlines, and budgets are met by the engineers and line workers.

In a small company the production manager is personally responsible for getting products boxed and delivered to the freight carrier on time, repairing equipment whenever it breaks down, and filling in for workers who call in sick.

Duties of a production manager at a *large* company:

- Ensures development of products in response to product-design specifications, as established by the general manager and the marketing and sales manager.
- Ensures a quality production process that meets established standards and achieves desired product yield from the use of raw materials.
- Ensures proper operation and maintenance of all production equipment in the plant.
- Ensures timely output of product in response to customer orders.
- Establishes procedures for the effective performance of production tasks and supervises staff in the execution of those procedures.
- Provides recommendations to the general manager for capital investments to maintain or improve the quality of the production process.
- Recommends improvements in marketing strategy and distribution policies or procedures.

Duties of a production manager at a *small* company:

- To ensure timely output of products, drags family to the plant on Saturday to pack crates and boxes and take them to the post office or parcel service if necessary.

- Visits hardware stores personally and places orders for tools and material.
- Inspects, by hand if necessary, everything that gets shipped in order to ensure quality.
- Repairs equipment, even on New Year's Eve if necessary, in order to ensure proper operation and maintenance of all production equipment in the plant.
- Establishes and writes procedures for the effective performance of production tasks and to supervise staff in the proper execution of those procedures.
- Comes up with new ideas for capital investments, marketing strategies, and distribution procedures.
- Posts notices of factory job openings at neighborhood community centers.
- Accepts the blame for any product that does not please either the president, general manager, manager of marketing and sales, or customer.

Swimming Lessons

A job in a small company might carry the small title as a job in a large corporation, but the actual daily activities and responsibilities that go with each job will be as different as pigs and polo ponies.

If you get bored doing one thing all the time and don't get flustered by distractions, you may like working in a small company. If distractions drive you to distraction and you need lengthy periods of solitude to focus on one problem at a time, you might hate working in a small company.

Your responsibility to yourself, and to your prospective employer, is to ask yourself which kind of person you are and to make sure that you find out what the president, or CFO, or marketing director of a small company really does during the day. When you switch to a small company, don't assume that just because your title stays the same, your job description will stay the same too.

Tips

❦ Find someone in a small company who will let you shadow him or her for a day, so that you see for yourself what a job in a small firm is like.

❦ There's never a dull moment in a small company. If you enjoy "keeping a lot of plates spinning" at the same time, you'll like working in a small company. If you'd like to be left alone to quietly do your thing most of the time, you may have the wrong temperament for a small company.

❦ Some executives really enjoy returning to a hands-on environment after years of delegating—they like rediscovering the feeling of accomplishing something themselves.

Part Two

Finding a Job in the Small-Business Market

Now that you know some of the characteristics of small companies, it's time to examine the techniques that can help you locate and win a job in a small company.

You'll use many of the same fundamental tools in a small-business job search as in corporate search. In both cases you must:

- Determine your skills, abilities, and preferences
- Write customized resumes and cover letters
- Tap your network and cultivate those who can help you
- Do research about companies you're interested in
- Present yourself well on interviews

Each of these activities, however, requires a different spin in a small-company search. You'll use different reference sources and you'll extend your network in different directions. Also, the weight of these activities—measured by the amount of time you dedicate to each of them—is distributed a bit differently when you're looking at small companies.

Networking, answering ads, and launching direct-mail or cold-calling campaigns, for instance, deserve greater attention in a small-company search. In a large-company search the use of executive-search firms and employment agencies would merit more of your time.

The relative effectiveness of various search techniques as well as the percentage of your time you should devote to each is as follows, according to the outplacement industry and to surveys of my workshop attendees:

	LARGE CO. (IN PERCENT)	SMALL CO. (IN PERCENT)
Networking	68	70
Responding to newspaper ads	9	15
Direct mail, telemarketing	8	12
Personnel services	15	3

Since you are most likely to find a job through your network, you must spend the majority of your time calling people in your network.

You will be broadcasting your new availability while focusing on the people who can give you information that might lead to your targeted job.

People who are changing careers or renewing old networks need time to explore new options and new sources of information. People who have been pushed into involuntary early retirement may need time to resolve their anger, self-doubt, and grief before they can search effectively for a new job.

Remember that a job hunt is not a linear process. Resumes do not always lead straight to interviews, and interviews seldom lead to jobs as quickly or as directly as we'd like. A job search is an upward spiral in which you gradually approach your goal. The dynamic of the search resembles the dynamic of the continuous quality-improvement process that so many businesses have adopted. By recording your progress and the success or failure of your efforts, you'll continuously improve your resume, your interviewing skills, and the quality of your networking.

At times you'll feel as though you're walking in circles. But if you follow the advice in the forthcoming chapters, you'll make upward progress. In the course of looking for a job, you will find new friends, discover more about the business world, and learn more about yourself.

CHAPTER SEVEN

Getting to Know Your Skills, Abilities, and Preferences

Before you can market yourself to a new employer, you must understand and evaluate yourself as a product. You have to ask, "What are my best qualities, traits, and characteristics? In what environment am I most comfortable? What kind of a person do I want for a boss?" In a small-company job search you must add one more question: "Would I be happy in a small company?"

The process of self-analysis involves tallying up your personal assets. The first type of asset is your *skills*. By that I mean your certified skills—expertise that you acquired in school or on the job and for which you have a certificate or degree that confirms it. The second type of asset is your *abilities* or *talents*, such as an ability to analyze difficult problems or to make people feel at ease.

The third category includes your *preferences*—the environment or culture that you'd most like to be in.

In my opinion your skills alone will often be enough to land you a job, but your abilities will determine whether you're really good at it, and your preferences will decide whether you're happy in it. To find the best possible job, you've got to become familiar with all three facets of your professional self. You won't be happy until your occupation meshes with your temperament and talents. The goal of career planning is to reach that place.

LEARNING MY SKILLS, ABILITIES, AND PREFERENCES

Getting there, however, can take years. In my own case it has taken most of my adulthood, and it's not over yet. Like many people I started out by acquiring external skills—college degrees and jobs that my degrees qualified me for. Later I began to appreciate my native talents and the wide variety of tasks they enabled me to tackle. And only very recently did I learn to respect my own preferences and allow them to guide me. Rather than being theoretical and trying to tell you how to know yourself better and how to understand your skills, abilities, and preferences more thoroughly, let me tell you how I did it.

Picking up basic skills

Like a lot of young people trying to plan their career, I chose a career and then figured out what skills I'd need to acquire in order to get the job I wanted. My choice was teaching (in the 1950s, women became either nurses, secretaries, or teachers), so I enrolled in an early-childhood education program at Wheelock College in Boston. Until then I had only known Far Rockaway, New York, where my family owned a small company that distributed snacks and novelties to New York's hundreds of corner candy stores. Small-business problems were the meat-and-potatoes of our family's suppertime conversations. But what

I was learning at home, even as it was shaping my talents and preferences, seemed unimportant at the time. Success would require specialized skills, which could only be found in college.

And, like most young women, I looked forward to creating a family. I fell in love with a West Point graduate during my senior year in college. After our marriage my husband's career took us to a series of cities. Eventually we landed in suburban Philadelphia, where my husband worked for General Electric and I taught elementary school. I was doing everything that a young woman in the mid-1960s was supposed to do.

My first recognition that happiness might require more than a diploma, a marriage certificate, and a job title came when my career plans collided with my family plans. After earning a master's degree. I was offered a tenure-track college teaching job and enrolled in a Ph.D. program at Bryn Mawr College. But at the same time pressures were building for me to become a mother. I was, after all, 26 years old. Feeling confused and ambivalent but anxious to do the right thing, I put my career on hold, and we had a wonderful daughter.

That was the beginning of the crisis that would lead me to discover who I really was. Of course I didn't know that at the time. All I could see in myself was failure. As a teacher I'd repeatedly gotten into hot water for breaking rules and challenging the principal's authority. My husband and I encountered difficulties that would eventually lead to a divorce. All of these problems seemed to be evidence of serious character flaws. I was unaware that I was growing and that my talents and preferences were pulling me in a new and positive direction.

Beginning to understand my broader abilities

After my divorce I became active in Women in Transition, a nonprofit social service agency created to help women like me cross that "no-man's-land" between wifehood and financial independence. Soon, as codirector of the group, I was busy raising money, hiring a staff, and lobbying at the state capital for reform of the divorce laws. In the process I was also learning that I had talents—or transferable skills, as we career counselors like to call them—that were independent of my college-certified skills.

An adviser to Women in Transition recognized my talents for organization and urged me to apply for her former job at ARA Services, the Philadelphia-based service conglomerate. I was soon managing a staff of ten, designing new benefits programs, and introducing wellness programs. Impatient for advancement, I took a human-resource management job at Sperry Corp. (now Unisys). A mentor saw that my abilities lent themselves to marketing and assigned me to set up a network of computer demonstration centers. I soon discovered that I was a natural "producer," or as Robert Reich puts it, "a strategic broker." I loved launching new projects.

When that assignment ended and I returned to a routine job, however, my sense of fulfillment waned. I wanted something that the average male-dominated Fortune 500 company couldn't offer. I preferred people over machines, teamwork over hierarchy, improvisation over policy, and diversity over homogeneity. I wanted something very different and smaller—something that would recall the best aspects of the small-business culture I'd grown up in. But I had no real appreciation—or respect—for these preferences yet.

Coming home to my true preferences

The first person to tell me that I had a right to follow my preferences was a venture capitalist named Fred Beste, the senior partner of NEPA Venture Fund in Bethlehem, PA. He was looking for people to run early-stage growth companies, and I answered his ad in *The Wall Street Journal.* During our interview something clicked. He enabled me to see that what I really wanted was to be involved in entrepreneurial ventures. More importantly, and I'll thank him for this forever, he urged me to, as they say, go for it.

Mobilizing my network

As it turned out, he didn't offer me a position. (Even the best interviews don't always yield a job.) But by adding the missing piece to the puzzle of my self-image, he enabled me, for the first time, to tell people exactly who I was and what I wanted. At subsequent job interviews I could say with confidence, "I want to start new projects in an entrepreneurial setting. I've worked in high-tech industries, I've done human resources and marketing. Do you need someone like me?"

The rest is history. I became a recruiter for embryonic companies in the University City Science Center, an incubator for early-stage high-tech firms in Philadelphia. I soon found myself in a lively, heterogeneous, entrepreneurial environment, working with people of almost every race, religion, nationality, and scientific discipline imaginable. In a sense it was Far Rockaway again—only bigger and better.

Finding my bliss

In January 1990 I left the Science Center to start my own executive-search and organizational consulting firm, CEO Resources Inc., and began to teach the job-search seminars that led to this book. Thirty years ago I could never have predicted that this is what I'd be happy doing. I didn't even know what a headhunter was. But as soon as I truly understood exactly what my skills, talents, and preferences were, it was almost inevitable that that self-knowledge would eventually lead me to the right career.

Swimming Lessons

What have I learned during the past thirty years that might help the job seeker in the small-company market? I've discovered that:

- *Most of us discount our strongest abilities because they come to us so naturally.* We take them for granted and overlook them.

We also frequently discount our preferences, because we believe that we don't deserve to indulge them. But our success in our careers often depends on whether we can identify our natural talents and find a job that stimulates them.

- *The more time you devote to understanding your own skills, abilities, and preferences, the less time it will take you to find the right job.* Many job seekers waste megawatts of mental energy contorting themselves into whatever shape they think an employer is looking for. You're better off if you decide what you want and what you can offer, and stick to it. As a headhunter I help my clients prepare a prioritized, detailed list of the traits they're looking for in a job candidate. As a job seeker you should create a list of your own criteria and look for a job that satisfies as many of them as possible.

- *It may take several job changes before you arrive at an employment "comfort zone."* Like myself many people spend years groping for their comfort zone. An acquaintance of mine from college, an actor and drama student, decided after graduation to train as a clown with the Ringling Brothers circus in Florida. He migrated to New York and helped create a successful musical based on the life of Fats Waller. Still unfulfilled, he landed a job in Washington, DC at the National Endowment for the Arts, where he helped budding artists find funds. He was in his element at last.

"I finally found someone who would pay to be myself," he told a friend. His previous jobs hadn't been digressions: each had furnished a necessary bit of preparation for his job at the NEA. Life, someone has surely said, is like sailing a boat into a headwind. To reach your goal, you'll have to tack back and forth a few times.

- *Many people unjustly punish themselves for not fitting into the big-company mold.* One of the people who attended my seminar, "How to Get a Job in a Small Company," was a very depressed executive who'd been outplaced several years before by a large company. Since his layoff he had earned a respectable living as an independent consultant in the utility financing field, but he felt relentlessly guilty about failing to "make it" in a corporation. "If others could adapt to the politics and the pressure," he said to himself, "why couldn't I?" He should have given himself more credit for the work he'd done as a consultant. There is life after the Fortune 500.

• *You can't explore your skills, abilities, and preferences without encountering the childhood experiences that shaped your character.* You don't have to be a psychoanalyst to know that we often re-create in the workplace the same interpersonal dynamics that we learned at home with our parents. Some people, I'm told, enjoyed perfect childhoods. But most of us must first defuse the unexploded bombs of our past before we can construct a satisfying future. In my case I had to unlearn many of the negative things I'd been told about myself. It took me years to recognize as strengths the traits I'd always regarded as weaknesses.

• *When people speak candidly about what they truly like to do, they make a much better impression.* By understanding yourself you become a better interviewee. At the beginning of my seminars I ask everyone to identify their occupation in terms of job history and basic skills. At the end of the seminar we repeat the exercise, but this time they all describe the aspect of their work that they most enjoy.

One woman, who at first had blandly described herself as a customer-service representative at a major computer manufacturer, eventually told us she truly enjoyed managing crises in which a customer's computer system had crashed 3,000 miles away and she had to orchestrate the technical support needed to get the system running again. As she warmed to her natural abilities, she became a very magnetic speaker and a more attractive future employee. (See Chapter Nine for a note on polishing your 60-second monologue.)

• *It's normal to wind up in a career that's only faintly related to the degrees you earned in college.* In my seminars I meet marketing people who started out in engineering, theater managers who started out in agriculture, cable TV people who started as economists, and fund-raisers who started out in English literature. One woman I know started as an accountant in the mergers and acquisitions department of a Fortune 100 company. Now, after discovering that she works best with people rather than numbers, she's head of marketing for a radio station.

• *It helps to ask others what they think your abilities and preferences are.* Assessing oneself is a risky business. Talk to a friend who works in a small company, and ask if he or she thinks you'd enjoy a small-business environment. During a long job search it's easy to lose perspective. Talking to a friend can help.

• *A career crisis is a life crisis that can propel you in one of three directions: up, down, or sideways.* Changing jobs creates a crisis. We can respond to it in one of three ways. We can stay the same. We can become depressed and decline into chronic anger and frustration. Or we can get to know ourselves better, grow, and come closer to finding satisfaction in our work and our life.

EXERCISES IN SELF-DISCOVERY

You may be able to define your skills, talents, and preferences more easily by writing down your most significant personal or professional accomplishments and then asking yourself a series of self-diagnostic questions about each one.

Following the samples on pages 123 and 124, try this:

• On a sheet of lined paper, write down 10 accomplishments that you are proud of. Don't stop until you've recorded all 10. They don't have to be on-the-job achievements. Feel free to jot down the volunteer work you've done or your academic achievements.

• Next to each of them write down your recollections of the accomplishment. Ask yourself, "What skills or talents enabled me to succeed in that situation? Did I enjoy the experience, and if so, why? Was I happiest when working with technical people or with literary types? Working indoors or outdoors? With abstract ideas or concrete objects? Alone or in collaboration? In an industrial or an academic setting?"

• Then take a fresh sheet of paper. Create a simple grid by listing your 10 favorite accomplishments horizontally across the

"Who Might Hire Someone Like Me?"

Assess yourself as a product, or as a family of products. Think about who might purchase you. Identify small companies that need exactly what you have to offer.

- *If you've just graduated from college,* a small company might hire you because they want to stay current with the latest technology and trends. To them you might be a walking continuing-education course.
- *If you're adept at turning new technologies into marketable products,* visit trade shows where inventors might have booths, venture fairs where early-stage companies look for investors, or one of the nation's business incubators or science parks, such as those in Evanston, IL, Philadelphia, PA, and Raleigh-Durham, NC.
- *If you speak a foreign language,* gather names of small international companies at lectures or seminars on export-import topics sponsored by Small Business Development Centers, World Trade Clubs, and branches of the World Trade Center Association, which are located in many major cities.
- *If you've spent many years as a manager at a large corporation,* offer your expertise and professional training to a small company that is struggling through the transition from "infancy" to "adolescence."
- *If you're a woman, older worker, or member of an ethnic minority,* find a company that wants to market its products to your demographic group, or a company operated by a woman, older person, or member of a minority.
- *If your goal is to remain in a certain geographical area,* present your familiarity with the local terrain as a selling point. A small company will save money on a relocation and won't have to worry that you'll move.
- *If you have an MBA* from a prestigious university, look for a small company that's about to make an IPO, or initial public offering. Your high-class credentials might help the company impress its investment bankers.
- *If you're a former schoolteacher,* use your communication and teaching skills to help a small company upgrade its public relations and training programs.

top of the page and listing 10 abilities vertically down the left-hand side of the page. The list of abilities might include negotiating skills, writing skills, teaching skills, facility with people, perseverance, diplomacy or humor. Any natural or acquired strength will do.

• Then fill in the grid by checking off the abilities that were demonstrated in each accomplishment. Look for patterns to emerge. Count the number of checks in each of the vertical columns. The more often you've checked off a particular ability, the stronger you perceive yourself to be in that area.

Very rarely do we assess our past experiences in a logical, objective way. We don't take the time to find out what made those experiences pleasurable or painful. But if you hope to change the future course of your life, you have to examine the past. By selecting your most important endeavors and studying why they were so satisfying or successful, you can begin to envision what your ideal job might be.

Tips

⚥ If you feel most comfortable in an informal, familylike atmosphere, a small company might be right for you. If you prefer
  prestige, security, and a hierarchical structure, you might stay
  in a large company or look for a small company with at least
  100 employees.

⚥ No matter what you may believe to be a personal drawback in
  the area of gender, age, race, religion, or physical characteristics, there will always be small-business owners who will like
  you the way you are.

⚥ Learning about yourself is integral to the search process. This
  is a journey to find your next best step, part of your continuous
  improvement process.

⚥ Change is never easy. And when you're forced to change, you
  will experience a rush of emotions, one of which will be anger.
  Unresolved anger will make you less effective as a job seeker,

MY ACCOMPLISHMENTS

1.

2.

3.

4.

5.

6.

7.

8.

9.

10.

because it will prevent you from presenting yourself in a positive light.

✖ Anger will also make you hypersensitive to the probing questions and the rejections that you will inevitably encounter from employers. Consult a therapist or career counselor for advice on growing past any of the emotions—fear, grief, depression, frustration, humiliation—that can accompany the loss of a job.

✖ Join a support group or meet with other people who share your predicament. You can learn many lessons about yourself, about your search, and about the job market from weekly or monthly meetings. Social isolation (the very opposite of networking!) is the last thing you need when you're looking for a job.

Your Ability Matrix

ABILITIES	ACCOMPLISHMENTS									
	#1	#2	#3	#4	#5	#6	#7	#8	#9	#10
a. *Negotiating Skills*										
b.										
c.										
d.										
e.										
f.										
g.										
h.										
i.										
j.										

CHAPTER EIGHT

Ten Personality Traits That Predict Success in Small Business

It takes a certain type of individual to thrive in a small-company setting. The temperament and abilities that make people successful in large companies don't necessarily work as well in small companies. As a result some people easily make the transition to small companies and make a big splash in a smaller pond. But others don't, and they run the risk of becoming fish-out-of-water when they move from a large organization to a small one.

No matter what your title or function, and no matter what kind of small business you eventually find work in, there are certain basic characteristics that will determine how successful you are. You may have flawless technical skills and years of experience in your industry, but to do well in a small company, you need a style that fits the needs of small companies.

I've identified ten basic characteristics that managers and executives in small companies need to exhibit in order to achieve success—both for themselves and for their companies. These qualities may not be readily apparent to someone reading your resume. Interviewers may never ask you specifically about them. But these are the intangible traits that small companies are generally looking for when they hire.

#1 The Swiss army knife trait

Like the famous red-handled knives from Switzerland, with their various blades, screwdrivers, corkscrews, and scissors, a manager in a small company must be highly versatile. People who can cope with a wide variety of assignments will usually do better in small companies than will the narrow specialist.

One of my clients started out as a writer in the marketing/communications department of a major sports magazine. She jumped to a 50-employee start-up that was trying to launch a new anti-inflammatory drug. Initially she wrote press releases and the annual report. But her responsibilities grew to include administration and human resources, which meant that she supervised the hiring process, benefits, shareholder relations, and general office operations.

Small companies always hope that the people they hire will soon take on more chores than they were specifically hired for.

#2 The rolled-up sleeves trait

At a small company you must be a "hands-on" employee. What does that mean? It means that you can survive without a secretary. It means that you can operate a personal computer and know enough about WordPerfect or Microsoft Word to write your own letters. If you're a CFO, it means you still know how to crunch numbers or keep books without having to have a junior accountant do it. In small companies the head of the department may be the *only* person in the department. You have to feel comfortable doing a variety of pedestrian chores.

For instance, one $15 million company was compelled by its contract with IBM to install a security-badge system for its employees. The small company couldn't afford to hire professional security guards, so the principals in the company took turns standing by the door at the beginning and end of the day and at the lunch hour to make sure that every employee was wearing an identity badge. Anyone who considers this type of chore beneath his or her dignity might not be happy in a very small firm.

#3 The decision-making trait

Because there are so few management layers in a small company, fewer people must sign off on any given decision. Consequently a manager has to make spot decisions much more often.

People who have worked only in very large companies become unaccustomed to making decisions themselves, or with a very limited amount of deliberation. They're used to referring decisions upward or letting a committee decide. Some people find it intimidating and disorienting to be forced to assess a situation and make a decision in a hurry.

Others will find the new freedom and the responsibility exhilarating. The pace of the business quickens when decisions are made more crisply. The decision makers are more likely to get direct credit—or blame—for what they've done.

#4 The "Gumby" trait

To work in a small company, you must be as flexible as Gumby, the animated clay character on children's television. In large companies change occurs at a slow pace. For small companies the caprices of the marketplace can wreak sudden, unexpected havoc. A new competitor may appear, a client may cancel a major order, a key employee may jump ship. Every day brings something new.

In one of the so-called Big Six accounting firms such as Arthur Andersen or Deloitte & Touche, for instance, a CPA might work with one client for several months. An accountant in a small or mid-market firm might work with several different clients a week, and each client will have its own unique temperament. Lawyers in small practices may see a wider variety of clients in a day than a corporate attorney will see in a year. In such cases the ability to adjust to changing situations is essential.

#5 The risk-tolerant trait

Because of their high failure rate, small companies require employees who can handle risk. A company like Du Pont can afford to carry an unprofitable division for years before deciding whether to beef it up, close it down, or sell it. But a small company is highly vulnerable to sudden shifts in the economy.

The average tenure at large companies, however, is shrinking too. Challenger, Gray & Christmas Inc., a Chicago-based employment consulting firm, reports that between 1984 and 1992, the number of years the average worker spends at a single job fell by nearly *half*—from 12.5 years to less than seven years.

#6 The scavenging trait

Are you a born bargainer? Would you feel comfortable haggling in a Middle Eastern bazaar? If so, you'll feel at home in a small firm.

At the typical large company, for example, the desks, the equipment, and the furnishings are all likely to be purchased new. At a small company those things are likely to be bought used. Small firm managers must be good at finding bargains and making fewer financial resources go farther. That means negotiating for good deals on office space, travel expenses, and insurance packages. The factory equipment itself may be purchased secondhand.

At one small company, managers became so obsessive about saving money that they bound their own notepads out of used computer paper rather than buy them at an office-supply store. When a big company goes to a foreign trade show, it hires a consulting firm to design, build, and transport its booth. A small company would be more likely to share a booth with another company, or piggyback on a U.S. government–sponsored mission. If it pains you to pay retail, your services will be valuable to a small firm.

#7 The "cuddling" trait

At small companies people reveal more of their personalities to each other, get to know each other better, and are more likely to develop relationships that are both personal and professional. The mere fact that there are fewer employees can foster deeper relationships. Discussions may range freely over a variety of personal as well as business issues. Anonymity and privacy are more difficult to maintain.

Individual departments of large companies can also be highly insular, but employees can wander to another department to make friends. In a small company you see the same faces every day and may choose your lunch companions from the same small group every day, not by choice but by necessity.

Personal problems are more likely to disrupt the social order in a small company than in a large company. In a family business the drama of the family is played out for all to see. The smaller the company, the more comfortable you must be with the other members of the team.

#8 The missionary trait

When you work for a small company, you "gotta believe" in the product because there's a good chance your customers have never heard of it. You must overcome their unfamiliarity with your fervent belief. Getting a foot in the door is tougher for the small-company salesman, so he or she has to be much more persistent, more persuasive, and harder to discourage than the

Could You Be Happy in a Small Pond? Take This Test.

Ask yourself the following 10 questions. The more times you answer yes, the more you'll enjoy life in a small company.

1. Could you tolerate not knowing where you might be working within two years?
2. Could you type your own letters and in other ways be your own secretary?
3. Could you work for a husband-and-wife team?
4. Are you a stickler for bargains?
5. Do you sleep as well in a budget motel as in a four-star hotel?
6. Would you enjoy lunching with the same bunch of people every day?
7. Can you pick up new skills on your own, without formal training?
8. Do you think of yourself as a Jack (or Jill) of all trades?
9. Are you comfortable hearing about others' personal problems at work?
10. Can you make a tough decision quickly and live with the consequences?

large-company salesman, who can simply whip out his company card and flash the familiar IBM or AT&T logo.

In a small company selling isn't limited to the sales force. Everyone, from the president who discusses the firm with his or her tennis partners to the receptionist who displays a winning smile to visitors, must be engaged in selling the company in their own way. They know that their own compensation depends on the company's performance in a much more direct and visible way than it would at a large corporation.

#9 The personal-commitment trait

Small-company owners often expect their employees to eat, sleep, and breathe the business and to work as many hours as they do. The late David Burpee, who ran the W. Atlee Burpee Seed Co. and made Burpee a household word to the millions of American gardeners who grew his company's giant marigolds and "Big Boy" tomatoes, was famous for ignoring weekends and took it for granted that his personal staff would do the same.

Large companies also expect long hours, but the commitment at a small company is even greater. When there are only 50 people on staff, the president knows whether you're behind him 100 percent or not.

#10 The quick-study trait

Big companies spend millions of dollars to train their upper managers. Small companies spend little, if anything, on training, and their managers often have to learn on the job or bring the knowledge with them. If you can't whistle the tune after someone else hums a few bars, you might feel uncomfortable at a small firm. New tasks are likely to be thrown your way at any time, and you must be able to respond in a hurry. Small firms will value the training that you received elsewhere and can pass on to others.

Tips

❖ The smaller the company, the greater the compression of responsibilities into a single job.

❖ Managing in a large corporation is 80 percent politics and 20 percent content. Managing in a small company is 20 percent politics and 80 percent content.

❖ Just as you don't buy a car in its first year of production, you shouldn't join an entrepreneur's first venture. Venture capitalists say that an entrepreneur's second or third attempt at starting a business is much more likely to succeed than the first one.

❖ No task is too big or too small for a small-company employer. Even the president may have to repair the copier if it breaks down.

❖ Small companies value people who have had specialized training at large companies and can pass that training along to their new colleagues at no cost to the company.

CHAPTER NINE

Weaving Your Small-Business Network

"Networking," says Robert Reich in his book *The Work of Nations,* is "the studied process of knowing what is happening and simultaneously making oneself known." We could add that networking for a small-company job means making oneself known to people who run small companies or know a lot about small companies. To find a job in small business, you have to tailor your networking strategy to people who have contacts in the small-business community.

An estimated 70 percent of all jobs are filled through networking. If anything, networking is more important in a small-business search than in a large-corporation job hunt. Small-business people don't have much time to look for new employees, and they rarely hire headhunters. Since they conduct their business on a more personal basis than the typical corporate manager does, they'd rather hire someone they know, or someone who has been vouched for by a friend. It's human nature: people want to hire people they can trust.

The art of networking has probably never been more important than it is today. The institutions that once tied people together and provided support in times of trouble—religion, family, and neighborhoods—have steadily frayed. Nor can we rely on either Uncle Sam or any large company to look out for us. Our best career safety net by far is the neural web of friends and colleagues who make a lifelong habit of sharing information and support with us.

Building and nourishing that web is the essence of networking. Networking means more than handing out cards at a card exchange or asking relatives if they know where you might find a job. It means identifying people who might help you, picking their brains, getting to know them, staying in touch with them, and doing favors for them with the faith that those favors will be repaid someday, somehow, by someone. Some people seem to have a knack for networking. But anyone can learn how to do it.

You may already be a subliminal networker. When you send holiday cards to old customers or suppliers, you're networking. When you call friends and ask them to recommend a dependable plumber, you're networking. When you attend a conference and introduce yourself to people who might help you, you're networking. When you host a "cocktail party" (as they used to be called), you're networking. When you systematically focus your energies on getting closer to people who possess information about growing small companies in your industry, then you're truly targeting the small-business market.

THE FOUR AXIOMS OF SMALL-BUSINESS NETWORKING

In networking for a small-business job, we find the following four truths to be self-evident:

1. *The smaller the business, the likelier it will hire through a networking contact.* Small companies seldom have human-

resource departments to handle their hiring, and they rarely use executive-search firms. At the same time, hiring mistakes are prohibitively expensive for them, and the intimacy of the work environment precludes hiring anyone who can't get along. So, to sleep better at night, small-company leaders prefer to find employees through their network.

2. *One good word from a third party speaks louder than a thousand words you can say on your own behalf.* Nothing opens doors like a personal referral from an intermediary whose opinion is trusted. It is the path of least resistance to a job. Just as a strong recommendation from *Consumer Reports* helps you decide which camera to buy, a strong recommendation will motivate a small-business person to meet you and interview you.

3. *Networking multiplies your efforts exponentially.* The more people you have putting out feelers for you, the broader the net you can cast, and the more quickly you'll track down a job. People who have enlisted dozens of other people in their job search find jobs a lot faster than those who search by themselves.

4. *The quality of your contacts is as important as the quantity of your contacts.* Spread your net wide at first and contact as many people as possible. But as your search progresses, focus your energies on the people most likely to lead you to the right job. At the same time, you must cultivate high-quality relationships with the most important contacts, by clarifying your own needs and being sensitive to theirs.

CASTING YOUR NETWORK

Before you start networking—that is, calling people on the phone, introducing yourself, and asking for information—you've got to focus your campaign, marshal your resources, and set goals. If you invest time in this now, you'll save time later on. The world of small business is too vast and too diverse to explore without a clear destination and a plan for getting there. You only have so much time and energy. Make it count.

- *Decide what kind of work you want to do, what skills you want to use, and where you want to work.* If you've done the preparation that's described in Chapter Eight, you'll have answered these questions already. If you haven't, please go back and reexamine your skills, abilities, and preferences. The more focused you are, the more quickly you will find people who can expedite your job search.

- *Decide what companies or market you're interested in.* Once you've determined what companies or which industries you'd like to work in, look for people who work or have worked for those companies or industries and can refer you to someone inside who has the power to hire you.

- *Toss out all the business cards left over from your last job and have new ones made.* They're essential for networking. Any print shop can produce such a card, which should contain your name, address, phone and fax number, and occupational specialty. But feel free to experiment. Consider using a double-sized business card, folded in the middle, that has room for a mini-resume on the back and a space for reminders.

- *Polish your presentation.* You must prepare a friendly, breezy, 60-second presentation that briefly describes who you are, what you do well, and what sort of information you're seeking. The chapters on interviewing and resume-writing also deal with the subject of the 60-second monologue.

- *Set networking goals.* Some people commit themselves to meeting one new person a day who might help in their job search. Others resolve to find at least one fresh job lead per week. Push yourself to talk to people and gather new information. Goals, even if not reached, will serve as incentives to keep plugging.

- *Develop a system—any system.* As each person you talk to refers you to two or three others, the size of your contact list will soon grow out of control. You need a system for logging each call, noting the result of the call, and reminding yourself when to call back again. Any system will do. But you must be religious about it.

"To whom can I turn?"

Talk to anyone who might have information about small companies. Talk to your barber or hairdresser, to your uncles, to your old colleagues. To avoid wasting time and energy, assign each prospect a level of priority.

"The first priority in my network," says one CFO, "was people who had lots of contacts with companies in my market. The second tier was acquaintances and people who I thought might let me know if they heard about something. One of them was a CFO in a leasing company. He knew what controllers or CFOs might be leaving other companies. The third tier was casual acquaintances and headhunters. But I talked to everyone. I left no stone unturned." Over a 7-month period he spoke to over 400 people, including 150 new contacts, before finding a job in a venture-backed surgical-products firm.

People from any and all of the following groups are worth making a part of your network:

• *Former colleagues, customers, suppliers, and salesmen who do business with small companies.* Countless people have gotten jobs through referrals from people they once worked with, if not as a co-worker, then as someone they traded with. "Salesmen I had met were my greatest source of leads," said one job seeker. "They know hundreds of companies."

Many of the people interviewed for this book found new jobs through former associates. One corporate executive found a job as COO of a small company started by a chemical engineer he'd worked with 12 years earlier. A young woman accountant from a Big Six accounting firm found a job as controller of a small company she'd audited. An ex-Hewlett-Packard engineer became vice president of marketing at a $3 million, 50-person computer firm that bought hardware from him when he was at H-P. Don't neglect to contact those whom you supervised in previous jobs.

• *Those who service small businesses, and who might help themselves by helping you.* That includes accounting and law firms, small banks, venture capitalists, computer dealers, marketing firms, advertising agencies, insurance agencies, and print shops. They work with small and medium-sized businesses every day on a person-to-person level. They'll be motivated to help you because they know that if they help you find a job, you're likely to buy their services in the future.

• *Anyone who works at a small company you'd like to work in.* If you've narrowed your job search to a handful of firms, ask your contacts if they or anyone they know works there. Current employees will possess exclusive information, not only about unannounced job openings but also about the company's culture and financial health.

• *People who have been in your shoes.* Those who have experienced unemployment firsthand often love to help somebody who has been outplaced. One 46-year-old research director who had been downsized out of a Fortune 500 company claims that some of his best leads came from near-strangers who had been in the same predicament: "A lot of my old business associates didn't come through. But then I came across a fellow I saw every two years at a trade show. I hardly knew him, but he'd been through a job search of his own, and he turned out to be my most valuable contact."

• *Friends, relatives, clergy, and neighbors.* Tell everyone in your personal or social network that you're looking for a job. These friends and acquaintances may have no influence in your industry, but they will probably have a strong desire to help you. One job seeker drafted a letter about his jobless status and sent a copy to all of the neighbors in his condominium development; he got eight job leads in return. Don't overlook old schoolmates. Most colleges and universities publish alumni magazines that contain news about job promotions or transitions among members of each graduating class. Get to know the alumni in your profession. You might even create a newsletter or an electronic bulletin board to stay in touch over the years.

Serendipity plays a big role in job search, just as it does in romance. You never know when or where you will meet someone who will introduce you to someone who introduces you to someone who can offer you a job. But serendipity is only part of it. As the saying goes, "We make our own luck," and the more you focus on a particular target in the job market, the luckier you will be. No wind favors a ship without a destination.

Go to where the people are

Willie Sutton, a famous New York City bank robber, was once asked why he robbed banks. "Because that's where the money is," he replied.

The same principle applies to networking. If you want to meet people in small business, you have to go where they go. Again, to save time, concentrate on events where you'll find people from small companies in your profession or in the region you want to live in. You'll meet them at:

• *Entrepreneurial and high-tech forums.* In most major cities and universities there are monthly or annual meetings where the owners or executives of venture-backed and high-tech companies meet to swap notes and meet potential investors. The New York Venture Group, for instance, sponsors a monthly $35-a-plate breakfast or luncheon where time is set aside expressly for networking.

• *Conferences and conventions in your field.* No matter whether you're a small-particle physicist or a collector of classic comic books, there's undoubtedly an annual convention that brings together hundreds of people who share your interests and who might know of companies that could offer you a job. One consultant in the utility-financing field cultivates his network by lecturing at conferences. By doing so, he avoids paying the $300 to $800 attendance fee. If you attend a convention to network, he advises, focus on networking. Don't become absorbed in the lectures.

• *Professional associations.* Groups like the National Association of Women Business Owners or the Regional Minorities Purchasing Council can put you in touch with countless small companies. Helping their members network is why these groups exist. *The Encyclopedia of Associations*, available at any public library, can furnish the names and phone numbers of national associations in your field.

• *Export groups.* Most major American cities have a World Trade Center Association office where small companies gather for information about exporting and importing. Many small cities have World Trade Clubs whose members meet monthly to dine, network, and listen to a guest speaker from the U.S. Commerce Department or a regional port authority.

• *Trade shows.* Every industry sponsors trade shows where you can exchange business cards with the executives of dozens of companies in your field. No matter what your field, there will be at least one annual show that virtually everybody in the field attends. Squeezed in among the big, showy corporate booths, you'll find a lot of small companies who have rented a few square yards of floor space and set up their own dog-and-pony show.

• *Electronic bulletin boards.* You can meet people in your field through electronic networks. On-line services such as CompuServe, Genie, Prodigy, Internet and others allow their subscribers to post job-search messages and requests for employment information on electronic bulletin boards. This is an excellent method for job seekers in high-tech fields.

It you're looking for a job in your own community and hope to familiarize yourself with a cross-section of local business people, you can meet them at:

• *Symphony, theater, and art-museum boards of directors.* If you live in a small city or town, try to join the board of directors of an orchestra, or the Boys and Girls Club, or a regional professional theater. Some of the most influential people in town use these boards to strengthen their own networks, and you can too. Pick an organization that interests you and ask someone to sponsor you as a director. If you volunteer your financial, marketing, or other practical skills, you'll probably be welcomed.

• *Support groups for people who are looking for work.* In church basements, public meeting rooms, and private living rooms all over the United States, unemployed professionals and managers now gather regularly to support each other in their job searches. These groups are useful not only for boosting morale but also for networking. Announcements of meetings often appear in local newspapers.

• *Chamber of commerce card-exchange events.* Even the smallest town has a chamber of commerce that publishes a directory that lists all of the members and vital information about each one. Most chambers sponsor events expressly to encourage networking.

• *Service organizations and social clubs.* Local business people can often be found at meetings of service organizations, such as the Rotary International, the B'nai B'rith, or the Association of American University Women.

• *Any public or private social function that you happen to attend.* You never know where you'll meet the person who will know about a job opening. In *Liar's Poker,* Michael Lewis's 1989 book about Salomon Brothers, he explains the way he networked his work into what at the time was the most successful investment bank in the United States. A recent Princeton graduate, Lewis happened to sit beside the wife of a Salomon managing director at a luncheon in London for the queen of England. They chatted, and she sent him to her husband for an interview. Lewis wound up making a six-figure income in his first year as a bond trader and then became famous with his kiss-and-tell best-seller about the inner workings of a Wall Street bank at the height of the 1980s financial boom. This isn't, of course, an example of small-business networking. But there are undoubtedly luncheons and banquets in your community where you can sit next to someone who can lead you to a job.

CREATING A WINNING PRESENCE

• *Play the host.* At public functions, "play the host" even when you're a guest. Be the first to introduce yourself and initiate a conversation. Better yet, think of yourself as a "network" television correspondent covering the floor of a presidential convention. Your job is to find the key people, buttonhole them, and ask them a few important questions.

I've found that women network more easily than men. Women are more accustomed to sharing feelings and information with each other. They're infinitely less "territorial" than men and are more inclined to nurture. People in marketing, sales, advertising—who are communicators by profession—seem to mingle more easily than people in finance, manufacturing, or engineering. But anyone can become a better conversationalist. The more often you deliver your 60-second infomercial, the more effortless it will be to strike up a conversation.

• *Use your network to help you approach the presidents of small firms.* If you know a "mover and shaker" in your industry, ask him or her to provide you with names of small companies in the same industry. With his or her permission draft a letter of introduction that appears to come directly from that person rather than from you. This will give you access to that person's network.

• *Use the telephone efficiently and effectively.* When calling people who know you only by referral, cut right to the chase. Offer a piece of information that will pique their interest in you. Demonstrate your knowledge of their business. To reach busy people, call early in the morning or late in the evening. That's when they're most likely to answer their own phone. To be more effective, take a hint from telemarketers. They smile as they talk and they close their eyes to block out distractions.

• *Be patient when networking.* When a good fisherman feels a nibble at the end of his line, he (or she) pulls back lightly to set the hook, then patiently pulls the fish in. A good networker fishes for information with the same sensitivity. Don't expect more help than any single person can give you. Be grateful for whatever information you can obtain.

• *Indulge your sense of curiosity.* You can often overcome shyness by drawing on your curiosity as a form of motivation.

BE AN ACTIVE RATHER THAN A PASSIVE NETWORKER

Networking isn't simply a euphemism for the old adage It's not what you know, it's who you know. Rather, networking means sharing information and building mutually beneficial relationships for the long haul. Here's how to do it:

• *Make deposits in the "Favor Bank."* In *Bonfire of the Vanities,* Tom Wolfe's satirical 1987 novel about Wall Street, greed, and the 1980s, he uses the term *favor bank* to describe a purely informal clearinghouse for favors that lawyers and other professionals and business people use in New York City. In other words, people actively perform unsolicited favors for other people with the implied understanding that at some undefined future date the favor will be returned—hopefully with interest. Don't expect a quid pro quo. Have faith that someone will return your good deeds.

It is essential to make regular deposits into your local favor bank. Networking is a two-way street. If you alert other people to opportunities that might benefit them, they will return the kindness by sending business or information your way. In fact networking reaches its highest potential when members of the network call each other to *offer* information without waiting to be asked. If you send business to your friends, they will gladly send you business when they can.

• *Follow up your contacts.* Remind people about yourself. "I had a notebook," says one job seeker, "where I logged every phone call I made, and I had a code where I wrote 'c/b' next to a name and number to remind me to call back. I kept track in my Day-Timer of my weekly and biweekly mailings and jotted down reminders to follow up the mailings with phone calls. After I spoke to someone, I ranked them either on the first, second, or third level of importance to my job search."

- *Make networking a habit.* Networking is more than a job-search technique. It's a way of life. Effective networkers network all the time. They weave friends and business associates alike into a vast safety net upon which they can fall in times of trouble. The best time to network is when you're still employed and have regular contact with customers, suppliers, and salesmen. Start networking *before* you enter the job market.

"I was too comfortable. I never joined any networking groups, because I never thought I would ever lose my job," says one woman, who was fired suddenly from a marketing job in the for-profit arm of a large, prestigious museum in Delaware after the woman who was her longtime friend, boss, and mentor was replaced by a man who failed to appreciate her years of loyal service. "But now I've learned."

- *Don't just meet people. Lead people!* Rather than simply attending conferences or joining organizations, became actively involved. Become an officer of a professional association. Offer to speak at a conference. Start a newsletter for peers and friends in your field. Create a job hot line. The closer you are to the inner circle, the more likely you'll be to hear useful information. Serving as president or vice president of an organization can exponentially increase your exposure to new people and new job leads.

THE PUSH-PULL THEORY OF NETWORKING

If you network long enough and hard enough, the members of your network will begin to reach out for you and will eventually "pull" you into a job. That's what happened to my friend Mike.

Despite having lost his CFO position at a high-tech start-up when the company's venture backers decided to "clean house," Mike felt cocky about finding a new position. Unpaid bills were already piling up, but he assumed that locating a new job would be as easy as calling a few old friends. "I'll have a job in three months," he told himself.

Months passed, however, and Mike ran out of old friends. So

12 Steps of Effective Networking

1. Develop relationships, ask for information or referrals—not a job or contract—find commonalities.
2. Create a prioritized list of target organizations, companies, and people.
3. Start with people with whom you are most comfortable.
4. Ask for feedback on your networking skills.
5. Pick referral sources that have a stake in your success.
6. Become active in at least three organizations.
7. Always have business cards.
8. Keep a data base of contacts, set goals, and measure your results.
9. Act like a host, not a guest, at gatherings.
10. Be opportunistic—every interaction is a potential networking opportunity.
11. Follow up regularly.
12. Continuously build new long-term relationships while constantly maintaining old ones.

he set up appointments with investors, accountants, and lawyers in the venture-capital community and asked them in a "nonthreatening way" if they knew of companies that might need him. Mike was building a network, but at the pace of a tooth extraction.

Then he had a breakthrough. A friend of a friend led him to a Saturday morning meeting at the home of a small-company CFO, who was wearing jeans and hammering together a deck behind his house. The CFO told him to go in the house, leaf through his Rolodex of business contacts, and pick any that looked interesting. Of 275 names, Mike picked 47. Of those he chose the most promising and phoned them to ask for more leads.

Though not a devout man, Mike could only describe what happened next as a "religious experience." As his name circulated within this new network, people began to seek him out.

"People I didn't know were willing to meet me, talk with me, offer suggestions," he says. "I'd get calls from people who'd say, 'I hear you're on a search. I've been through it, and I want to wish you luck.' That happened a half dozen times. I once received tips from three or four people about the same job, and a guy called to alert me to a job that hadn't been advertised yet."

Most surprising of all, he discovered that strangers would do favors for him to thank those who had helped *them* in the past. "It was like karma," Mike said. "One guy told me, 'I can't help the person who got me a job, so this is my way of paying him back.' "

He had discovered networking's true power: its liquidity. Networks, in other words, are the open markets on which favors are exchanged between strangers who have a friend in common. "You don't really understand until you've been through it," Mike says.

Mike's experience also demonstrated that the push-pull theory of marketing applies to networking. This theory posits that if you push the right product hard enough and long enough in the right segment of the marketplace, the market will eventually pull the product from you. The secret is not to quit before you reach that point of escalating returns.

What finally happened to Mike? He called a colleague from the distant past, who sent him to a venture-backed company that was interviewing for a CFO. Ten grueling interviews and three months later, Mike was offered the job. His conversion to networking, needless to say, is wholehearted. "If I hear of a job opening, I feel almost obligated to call someone in my network," he says. "Just to prove that it really works."

Maintaining Your Momentum

You're bound to experience frustration when your networking efforts don't produce immediate results. Here are some of the most common obstacles that crop up in networking, and some suggestions on how to cope with them:

• *"I don't know anyone."* Unless you've been a hermit for the past ten years, you undoubtedly know more people than you think you do. Networking works like a pyramid: Your first contact leads to two more, and those two lead to four new ones, and so forth. *Remember that you're tapping into other people's existing networks.* Once you break in, the referrals will come more easily.

- *"I can't just call people I don't know."* If you're shy, start out by calling people that you feel comfortable with, and don't call strangers until you feel confident. Keep in mind that calling people is easier if you find a way to offer them information in addition to asking for some.

- *"I've run out of momentum."* To stay motivated, develop goals and a system for reaching them. The best networkers push themselves to accomplish something specific every week. But if you're truly tired, take a rest. Recharge your batteries. Better to rest than to send out negative energy.

- *"I don't want my current employer to know I'm looking for a new job."* If you must keep your job search a secret, ask other people not to use your name when they make inquiries on your behalf. But don't keep yourself a secret forever. Eventually you will have to take the risk that your intentions will be known.

Swimming Lessons

Your network is your occupational safety net. The people in your network constitute a vast part-time sales force that's helping you market yourself. They're the best form of unemployment insurance that money *can't* buy. We live in a society where many of the old structures, such as church and family, have been weakened for many people. Fewer and fewer large corporations can offer the sense of long-term security they once did. Our networks are what we have instead. To quote the Beatles, "We get by with a little help from our friends."

Successful networkers network routinely, whether they're searching for a new job or not. Like fishermen, they mend their nets every day. They *turn to* their network when they need a job rather than waiting until they lose a job to start networking. They network actively rather than passively, helping to create events rather than merely attend them. They do favors for others, trusting that those favors will be returned. They leverage their networking efforts by joining networks that already exist.

At its best, networking can be an adventure. It is an excellent way to meet people in your community. By networking you'll not only expand your circle of professional contacts. You'll expand your circle of friends. In fact your contacts will become your friends. And vice versa.

Tips

☙ Send out a newsletter that alerts people in your network to the state of your job search. It will keep your face in front of them without wearing out your welcome.

☙ Small business people rely on their networks to send them people with the right temperament. "I need to know if they can handle not only the good days around here but also the bad days, when vendors or customers call with problems, and everyone's in your face. I can find that type of person most quickly through networking," said one president of a metal-pipe company.

☙ Approach networking with a spirit of fun. People respond more enthusiastically to networkers with upbeat attitudes.

☙ The paradox of networking is that you can safely predict that you'll find your next job with the help of your network, but you can't predict who in your network will lead you to it.

☙ There's an old saying in politics: "Don't take nobody nobody sent." It means that no one gets admitted to the inner circle unless a member of the inner circle vouches for them. The same principal holds true in a job search.

☙ Networking reaches its highest potential when members of the network call each other to *offer* information without waiting to be asked for it.

☙ Offer information, don't simply ask for it. When you talk to people over the phone or at a public function, find out what they do and tell them something that might be helpful to them. They will be all the more motivated to offer information to you.

- To overcome shyness at a public event, remind yourself that the other people in the room—merely by their presence—have shown that they share your interests. You will naturally have a lot in common with them—and a lot to talk about.

CHAPTER TEN

Gathering Information About Small Companies

High among the crags of the Absaroka mountain range in southwest Montana, there's a small alpine pond where golden trout swim in abundance. If you try fishing for goldens in any of the other lakes or ponds located in that part of the Rockies, you won't find them. But if you hike the two miles up a steep rocky trail to this obscure little lake and use the right bait, you'll bring home a creel full of rare golden trout.

A search for a small company job demands a similar specificity of focus. Unless you define what you're looking for, you'll waste a lot of effort fishing in unproductive waters. By now, you've probably completed the tasks of identifying what you want to do (see Chapter Seven) and who might help you (see Chapter Nine). Now it's time to use the library to research the names, addresses, and vital characteristics of small companies you might like to work for.

Luckily we live in the Information Age. The world virtually sloshes in data, much of it regarding small companies. There are directories and on-line data bases of fast-growing small companies, encyclopedias of associations that small companies might belong to, tomes on the credit-worthiness of small companies, reference books where companies are indexed by location and industry, and countless trade magazines that carry valuable ads and features about dynamic small companies. The task of collecting and distributing this information has become an industry in itself.

In the past, marketers and investors have mined this mother lode of facts to locate the best companies to sell their products to or to buy shares in. You're managing your career like a business, so you should use this same information to decide where to market your skills and where to invest the next several years of your life.

Many of the books, magazines, and data bases you need can be found in any good public library with the help of a reference librarian. Additional information can be tapped electronically from a variety of new on-line data bases, either with the help of an independent information broker or through your own personal computer and modem.

Remember that these research techniques are meant to *complement* your networking efforts. Research methods and networking methods are two ways of reaching the same goal from opposite directions. When you network, you meet people who can alert you to good companies. When you conduct research, you're locating names of companies whose managers you'd like to meet. Once you've drawn up a list of target companies, you'll need to network your way to the people who run them. Search methods and networking go hand in hand.

HIE THEE TO A LIBRARY!

Many libraries have developed special programs or departments that not only help job seekers find the names and addresses of small companies in their field but also help them evaluate the financial outlook of just about any company and any industry. You can use the library to:

- Find out which industries promise the greatest growth
- Find out which professional or trade magazines cater to those industries
- Learn the names of companies in those industries
- Learn about the financial health and prospects of those companies
- Gain access to magazine and newspaper articles about specific companies

WHERE TO FIND GROWTH INDUSTRIES

Most libraries have reference books where you can find forecasts and predictions of growth in various sectors of the economy and specific industries. If your search is very broad and you want to get into a hot field, the following books can help you:

Predicasts Forecasts. This quarterly report gleans other publications for data on the short- and long-range outlook for products and business activities.

Standard & Poor's Outlook. This weekly periodical analyzes the previous week's stock trading and its impact on the future, discusses investment opportunities, and analyzes both industries and specific stocks.

Standard & Poor's Industry Surveys. An investors' quarterly that discusses investment outlooks and statistics on 22 industry categories.

Trendline's Current Market Perspectives. An investors' weekly that analyzes short- and long-term trends for over 1,400 stocks.

Value Line Investment Survey. Weekly analyses of 1,700 companies and 76 industries.

U.S. Industrial Outlook. A U.S. government annual forecast of the prospects for more than 350 manufacturing and services industries, plus the names and phone numbers of the experts who wrote the analyses.

Occupational Outlook Handbook. Listings of careers, industries, and their prospects for growth.

FINDING THE RIGHT PROFESSIONAL OR TRADE JOURNAL

For virtually every industry and profession there are magazines that include articles on trends and specific companies, advertisements that publicize jobs and growing companies, and, often, annual indexes of the hottest companies in the field. To find them, look in the following directories:

Encyclopedia of Associations. Thousands of trade associations are indexed by subject and keyword, and entries supply the name of any periodical the association publishes.

Standard Periodical Directory. A compendium of U.S. and Canadian periodicals, indexed by subject and title.

National Trade and Professional Associations of the United States. Same as above.

Standard Rate & Data Service. Names of a wide range of newspapers and magazines, indexed by title and subject.

Gale Directory of Publications and Broadcast Media. Names of trade publications indexed by city and subject.

Your library may already receive the periodical that interests you. To subscribe, call the telephone number listed in the directory. You can judge the magazine's usefulness by who writes the articles, what the articles are about, who publishes it, who advertises in it, and whether the magazine carries items such as classified employment ads and calendars of networking events.

Look for magazines that cover your *industry*, such as electronics, waste management, or health care, as well as those that cover your *function*, such as marketing, human resources, or engineering. Ask people in your industry which professional magazines they read. If you're conducting a local search, read the local business tabloids.

Look for Magazines that Publish Business Directories

Many specialty business magazines publish annual directories of small, growing companies. Those published by *Inc.*, *Forbes*, *Business Week*, and *International Business* magazines are among the best known, but state, regional, and local business periodicals also carry directories. Some states have technology councils that publish glossy quarterly magazines that print directories of, for instance, all of the small software companies in the state.

Many metropolitan and suburban business tabloids publish lists of the 100 fastest-growing small companies in their circulation areas. The entries in each directory will include some or all of the following data: the name of the company, its industry, annual sales, number of employees, address, phone number, fax number, the name of the CEO or president, and rate of growth.

Check the Employment Tabloids

To cover all of your bases, you should check into the three national newspapers that are dedicated to help-wanted ads. They are:

National Business Employment Weekly, a weekly compendium of classified and feature ads for jobs at large and small companies, published by Dow Jones & Co. Inc. and available at most newsstands and libraries.

Employment Review, a tabloid published monthly by Recourse Communications (334 Knight Street, P.O. Box 1040, Warwick, RI 02887. 401-732-9850, fax: 9856). It carries large numbers of advertisements for jobs at small and mid-sized technology firms throughout the United States. Each issue also contains a calendar of networking events, support-group meetings, and seminars, all catalogued by geographical region. Subscription price: about $40 a year.

National Ad Search, a publication that gathers want ads from 75 major newspapers every week. Each issue contains over 2,300 ads in 55 fields. Some libraries carry it, and a six-week subscription costs $40. For information call, 800-992-2832.

How to find names of employers, by industry

You can find out a lot about companies by looking them up in one or more of the directories that can be found in the reference section of most public libraries. Some are general and include all kinds of employers, while others are specialized, listing employers by product or service.

Some of the best general directories are:

Standard & Poor's Register of Corporations. Basic information on more than 45,000 public and private companies.

Harris Directories. A series of state-by-state directories containing the names of all manufacturing companies indexed by name, geographical location, SIC code, and product. Entries include names of key executives, sales, plant size, export or import status, ownership, and type of computer used.

The Dun & Bradstreet Reference Book of Corporate Managers. Contains biographical information on officers and directors at more than 12,000 U.S. companies.

Dun's Directory of Service Companies. Contains basic information on U.S. service companies.

Dalton Directory. Offers the name, address, product, names of officers and managers, and approximate number of employees of firms in a given geographical area.

Some excellent specialized directories are:

Thomas' Register of American Manufacturers and *Thomas' Register Catalog File.* Provides information on manufacturers, suppliers, and distributors.

Standard Dictionary of Advertising Agencies. Lists more than 4,000 U.S. advertising agencies.

Directories in Print. A guide to over 14,000 published directories, divided into 26 broad subject areas, with subject, title, and keyword indexes.

Chamber of commerce and other local business directories. Small companies comprise most of the membership of chambers of commerce; many may be too small for your needs.

Directory of Executive Recruiters (Kennedy Publications). An annual listing of thousands of executive recruiters throughout the United States, indexed by geographical location.

HOW TO FIND ARTICLES ABOUT SMALL COMPANIES OR INDUSTRIES THAT INTEREST YOU

Many libraries now have computer terminals (INFOTRAC) where you can type in the name of the topic, individual person, or company that interests you and receive a screenful of references to pertinent articles in various magazines and newspapers.

At a large urban library this data base might include a general periodicals index of hundreds of magazines and newspapers, the *Business Periodicals Index* (also available in print), the *National Newspaper Index* of the major metropolitan newspapers, and a general business file of company reports, references to trade journals, and company names.

RESEARCHING PUBLIC COMPANIES

Some libraries collect the annual reports of companies in their region. Profiles of publicly traded companies can also be found in:

Standard & Poor's Corporation Records. Financial reports on companies listed on major as well as regional stock exchanges; updated quarterly.

Standard & Poor's Stock Reports. Entries include 10-year financial histories; updated quarterly.

Moody's Handbook of Common Stocks. Basic information, including officers and capital structure, on publicly traded companies; analyses of 1,000 companies of high investor interest.

Moody's Industrial Manual. Similar to *Moody's Handbook,* but not limited to stock companies.

WRITING TO SMALL COMPANIES

Once you have the address of a publicly owned company, you can write to its shareholders' relations or public relations office and request a 10-K form. Public companies are required by the U.S. government to publish these forms, which list the current activities of the company, often in great detail.

Privately held companies aren't required to file a 10-K form. Less information in general is available about these closely held firms, since they do not solicit investment from the public. A private company may be glad, however, to furnish you with an annual report or promotional material.

ON-LINE DATA BASES

As more and more Americans own personal computers, the number of on-line data bases that are available to them via modem has mushroomed. A few of these data bases are full of job openings, company profiles, and trade-show schedules.

Beware, however, that using the data bases from your home computer can be expensive and sometimes requires advanced computer skills. A good public or university library may provide access to on-line data bases free of charge or may have the information on file or on microfilm.

Business American Online (402-593-4593). This Iowa-based data base, new in 1993, contains the names of hundreds of thousands of businesses, indexed by industry, number of employees, revenue, zip code, and rate of growth. More importantly, it includes a file of 12,000 companies with an annual growth rate of 20 percent or more, as a well as a file of small-business owners. Information on 90 percent of the businesses in the United States is updated monthly. Anyone with a PC and a modem can access the data base for $1 a minute and 20¢ per lead.

Tradeshow Week's Custom Data Service (310-826-5696). Tradeshow Week in California, a trusted source of information on trade shows for the past 20 years, has made its data base available to the public. For $25 you can receive the dates and locations of three or four major trade shows in your industry during the coming year. Additional leads cost $2 per show.

Orbit (800-955-0906). This information distributor handles the data base of 35,000 high-tech companies nationwide of Corporate Technology Information Services, Inc., Woburn, MA. Cost of subscription, $50 per year, plus about $2 per minute per search. Data are updated quarterly.

Military Business Alliance & Association (212-619-2618). This organization maintains a data base of temporary and permanent jobs for veterans and a data base of resumes for employers.

The Army Employer Network Database (800-445-2049). This data base, available at 55 Army Career Alumni Program offices worldwide, includes on-line want ads posted by more than 3,000 companies.

E-Span JobSearch (800-682-2901). A PC data base of 1,500 professional and technical job openings, updated weekly, at large and small companies, that can be accessed through on-line vendors such as Prodigy.

Lexis-Nexis. Full-text articles and entries from newspapers, magazines, directories, and clearinghouses. Accessible at university and law school libraries.

Businesswire and PR Newswire. Data bases of press releases and short articles about both public and private companies.

Hot spots, or "symbolic-analytic zones"

Certain regions of the United States offer more opportunity than others, especially for those with high-tech skills. In 1992 *Business Week* magazine identified 16 cities where there were a total of 600,000 high-tech jobs. Robert Reich calls such robust areas symbolic-analytic zones, because so many of the people who work in them earn their living by analyzing and manipulating symbols and ideas rather than by producing traditional goods and services.

These areas, along with their principal industry and number of high-tech jobs, include:

Tucson, AR: 40 companies, 1,000 jobs; lasers and electro-optics

San Diego, CA: 163 companies, 11,000 jobs; biotechnology, communications

Washington, DC: 1,100 companies, 80,000 jobs; systems integration

Orlando, FL: 35 companies, 5,000 jobs; lasers and electro-optics

Boise, ID: 25 companies and 14,300 jobs, focused on the semiconductor-chips and laser-printer industries

Champaign, Urbana, IL: 63 companies, 3,500 jobs; software

Hunt Valley, MD: 400 companies, 15,000 jobs; software and medical technology

Minneapolis and St. Paul, MN: 500 companies, 40,000 jobs; medical instruments and health care

Princeton, NJ: 400 companies, 132,400 jobs; biotech and telecommunications

Corning, NY: 110 companies, 31,500 jobs; ceramics and electronics packaging

Plymouth Meeting, PA: 500 companies, 166,000 jobs; bio-tech research and medical products

Austin, TX: 450 companies, 55,000 jobs; computer manufac-turing and chips

Richardson, TX: 500 companies, 50,000 jobs; telecommuni-cations systems, software

Provo, UT: 175 companies, 12,000 jobs; software

Salt Lake City, UT: 75 companies, 8,000 jobs; medical devices and artificial organs

WHY HOT SPOTS ARE WHERE THEY ARE

Hot spots occur where innovative technologies, highly edu-cated people, and lots of money converge. Growth in these are fostered by the following: (a) a coalition of large companies that act as sources of capital and technology for small companies and use them as suppliers; (b) one or more well-funded research universities; (c) a state government that provides seed capital to high-tech start-ups; and (d) a network of venture capitalists.

Notice that neither Silicon Valley in California, nor Route 128 in Massachusetts, two of the hottest hot spots for the computer industry in the 1980s, are listed above. That's because the location of hot spots can change unexpectedly. When one area cools off, a new hot spot appears somewhere else. But there will always be technological "gold-rush towns" somewhere in the country. Try to locate the hot spot in your field.

Swimming Lessons

You may be overwhelmed by the sheer number of places to look for employment information. Keep in mind that each of these information sources will not necessarily lead you in a different direction. They are merely different routes for arriving at the same place. Pursue any or all that are available.

Research methods work best when combined with networking.

In networking, which should take up 60 or 70 percent of your time, you will focus on finding people. In researching, which should occupy about 30 percent of your time, you will focus on finding companies. Research and networking techniques are complementary ways of reaching the same goal from opposite directions.

Tips

❊ Talk to your librarians. They are quite willing to help you find the books and magazines you need. Ask for the research librarian or, in a large library, the business or career research librarian.

❊ Do your research at a college library and dress like a business person. There won't be many other adult job seekers there, and the librarian will offer you special attention because you'll stand out among the students.

❊ To find an independent information broker who can conduct data-base research for you, look in the *Directory of Fee-Based Information Services*, published by Burwell Enterprises, Houston, TX.

CHAPTER ELEVEN

Customizing Your Small-Business Resume and Cover Letter

Small-company owners and CEOs are skeptical of resumes, because they feel that job seekers can always hire someone to write their resumes for them. Many bullfrogs, surprisingly, claim they rely on the cover letter to get a feel for the human being behind the resume. A resume that seems "polished" to a corporate interviewer may merely sound "canned" to the small-company executive.

A sparkling resume, cover letter, and thank-you notes alone won't land you a job. You'll need networking, perseverance, and luck for that. But your written communications can showcase your intelligence, wit, honesty, and attention to detail while demonstrating to a CEO why you're right for his or her small business.

So when you write a letter or resume, make it count. It's your bait, so to speak, when you fish for a job in a small pond.

A resume can serve an additional purpose. The very act of writing it forces you to reconsider where you've been, where you are, and where you'd like to go. It also boosts your morale by forcing you to recall all the positive things you've done but took for granted and never gave yourself enough credit for.

Too many people, I find, make the mistake of producing a resume that reads like a tombstone—a lifeless record of their past, without a hint of their plans for the future. In addition to summarizing your past, the resume should be an assertion of how you envision your future.

More to the point, since you're managing your career like a business and marketing yourself like a product, your resume should accomplish what any good marketing brochure accomplishes: It should demonstrate your features, your functions, and most of all your benefits to the buyer. Above all, keep it brief—one page if possible, two pages at the very most—and make sure that the most important information stands out clearly from the rest. Bear in mind that the attention span of the average American has been shrinking ever since television was invented.

There is no single correct method for writing a resume. If you're looking for a specific model or template, there are dozens of books that provide such things. What you will find here are general principles that will help you craft the kind of resume that a small-business person is most likely to respond to.

A RESUME BUILT ESPECIALLY FOR SMALL BUSINESS

If you're changing careers, or shifting from a large company to a small one, or just reentering the work force after college or child rearing, or switching from a nonprofit or public-sector organization to a private-sector job, then you might use what I call the semifunctional resume.

A semifunctional resume combines the best elements of a traditional "chronological" resume, which emphasizes your employment history, and the much trendier "functional" resume, which highlights your transferable skills (such as marketing, finance, or research) and your natural abilities (such as analysis, entrepreneurship, or management).

After your name, address, and phone number, the outline of a semifunctional resume would contain the following items (see also the sample resume on pages 174–175):

Objective
Summary Statement
Functions
Chronological Work History
Education
Personal Information

TELL THEM WHAT YOU WANT

Small-business owners are looking for people who fit in perfectly with the demands and culture of their companies, and if your "objective" statement matches their objective, you'll probably get an interview.

People often ask, "Should I customize my resume to each application?" Absolutely. Today's word processors make it a snap to crack out endless variations. Adapt the objective to the job you're seeking.

The objective statement, which should appear on both your cover letter and your resume, will tell the reader the level of authority you've reached or hope to reach (general manager, professional, entry level), your field (marketing, financial, graphic arts), the industry you're targeting (manufacturing, electronics, publishing), and the desired size of the company and geographical location (usually the size and location of the firm to whom you're tailoring the resume).

The objective can also describe your chosen specialty (for example, bringing new inventions to market, turning around troubled companies, preparing a company for an initial stock offering, and so forth).

Here's an example of a good objective statement:

> A *marketing management position using strong analytic, operations, and business-development skills in a small or mid-sized high-growth service company in the San Francisco Bay Area.*

Although the "objective" appears near the top of the resume, write it last. You may not have a clear idea of your objective when you first sit down to draft your resume. You may need time to review your career, interests, and goals first. Your objective will vary in response to new and unexpected opportunities. Forcing yourself to clarify your objective is one of the side benefits of writing a resume.

SUMMARIZE WHY YOU'RE QUALIFIED TO PURSUE YOUR OBJECTIVE

If you are changing careers or industries and your job history doesn't match your new objective—for instance, if you've had your own management-consulting practice but want to specialize in marketing at a small firm—then you must write a bridge paragraph that explains why you are qualified to pursue your new objective.

This paragraph is your "summary statement" or "professional profile." It should describe the package you can offer the target company. Here's an example:

> A *management professional with eleven years' experience, seven as a principal in the marketing or planning departments of large manufacturing companies and four years as a small-company turnaround expert in a management-consulting firm.*

This statement allows you to support your objective in clear, simple language. If your job history doesn't fully support your objective, the skills statement can bridge the gap. If you hope to change careers, by all means say so and offer evidence to support your claim that you can do it. Use this opportunity to craft the image that you'd like to convey.

A word of caution: Some small-business CEOs, especially those in manufacturing and engineering, break out in a rash when they read skills statements or professional profiles that are gushy or nonspecific. Adjectives such as *resourceful, hardworking*, or *results-oriented* are unconvincing unless they're followed up with supporting evidence. In any case, be as specific as possible in describing yourself. Ask yourself, "Exactly what type of hired gun am I? What do I do really well? How can I make myself sound unique?"

BENEFITS YOU CAN OFFER THE BULLFROG

This is where you list your functional experience, your talents, or your accomplishments. Emphasize the traits that bullfrogs look for, such as versatility and quick decision-making ability. In the sample resume on pages 174–175, the job seeker listed three separate functions or talents while supporting each claim with examples of achievements at previous jobs. For example:

Business Analysis. Resourceful, customer-driven analyst with a keen ability to focus on key issues, who thrives on variety and challenges. Grounded in financial results with strong communications skills.

- Instituted changes to improve communications, quality assurance, and employee satisfaction in a multi-divisional service firm with growth in excess of 200 percent over three years
- Facilitated the change to a customer orientation for a specialty chemical manufacturer

- Revitalized a manufacturer in a mature market to achieve profitability and 50 percent growth.

TAILORING YOUR JOB HISTORY TO THE SMALL-BUSINESS EMPLOYER

Next comes the list of jobs you've held, your titles (if they're impressive and relevant), the names of the companies you've worked for, and the dates of your tenures there.

All employers, of course, like to see steady progress up the success ladder, with a minimum of job hopping or unexplained absences from the job market. If you've changed jobs every two years, find a way to deemphasis that fact. Underplay the dates of your arrival and departure, or indicate that each job was a promotion, or demonstrate that you stayed in the same field despite frequent job changes.

If you've worked at a large company, resist the temptation to boast about how many legions of workers you supervised and how many billions of dollars in sales your department racked up. If you were so important, the small-business person may wonder why you're looking for work. Be prepared to demonstrate that you can be effective without a big team or big budget behind you.

If you've only served in volunteer organizations—this might be true of a woman returning to the work force after raising children—include them on your resume as though they were paying jobs. If you raised an impressive amount of money for an art museum or led a marketing campaign that doubled an orchestra's ticket sales, by all means toot your own horn. People in nonprofit organizations know as much about "doing more with less" as small-business people do.

IF YOU'VE GOT IT, FLAUNT IT

Ordinarily your academic credentials would appear near the bottom of your resume. But if your degree is your strongest suit,

Different Summaries for Large and Small Companies

Here's how an executive described himself in the resumes that he used when applying for a job at a large corporation:

"Successful manufacturing executive who has enjoyed a career with two highly respected Fortune 500 companies. Experienced in management of plants and technical services of engineering, quality assurance, and product development. Skill in managing union and nonunion employees. Results-oriented manager with excellent interpersonal and communication skills."

Here's how we changed his resume to suit the small-business job market, without changing any of the facts, merely emphasizing the facts that might appeal to a small-business employer:

"Successful operations executive who has developed and turned around plants ranging from 200 to 500 employees. Experienced in all aspects of manufacturing and finance with hands-on experience recruiting and retaining hourly workers, installing MRP Systems, and designing and conducting training on Total Quality Management."

you may move it to the top of the resume. On one resume the job seeker's name appeared at the top center, flanked on the left by her address and on the right by the name of her college. Since her M.A. from Yale University was the most eye-catching item on her resume, it made sense to display it prominently.

Another woman sold herself short by burying her master's degree on the second page of her resume. Since her job history was weak—she was returning to the workplace for the first time after 20 years of homemaking—she should have made her educational history more conspicuous.

If you do not have a degree but have many accomplishments, hide your educational history on the second page. Mention any partial schooling or professional training you may have had.

Remember, many small-business people are often reverse snobs and may prefer those who are self-educated.

PERSONAL DATA THAT SUPPORT YOUR OBJECTIVE

This section offers an opportunity to reveal the real person behind the resume. Include here any leisure-time activity that might make you a more desirable candidate, support your objective, and overcome any objections or prejudices that the interviewer might have.

If you are older and want to dispel any notion that you might be ready for a rocking chair, mention that you're an avid tennis player, golfer, or jogger (if you are, that is). Mention any leisure-time activity that supports your career objective.

Feel free to mention awards you've won, professional organizations you've belonged to, or civic groups you've served in.

While it's safe for a man to say he's married with children, women shouldn't always do so. Some employers still worry that a woman's responsibilities to her family will distract her from the single-minded pursuit of success on the job.

CREATIVE FORMATS, PRO AND CON

To make their resumes more conspicuous, some people use more unusual formats.

One job seeker bent on making the transition from the nonprofit sector to a private-sector firm converted his resume into a list of pairs of "Problems" he'd been faced with at work and "Solutions" he'd come up with. He wanted to compensate for the belief among some small-business executives that people in nonprofit businesses aren't bottom-line oriented. He eventually got a top marketing position in a successful health care consulting firm.

Similarly, a speech writer presented his resume in the form of a speech, using the same format he'd use if he were submitting an actual draft of a speech for a CEO to deliver at a banquet. A woman who hoped to join the marketing department of a national sports magazine went to the trouble of finding out that the magazine's marketing theme for the year was "Recipes for Success." Every week she mailed the editor a new "recipe" for success, indicating what she would do to expand circulation. She got the job.

Another person, applying to a supermarket chain, printed his resume on one of the chain's own brown-paper grocery bags. One fellow who applied for a project-management job put his resume in the form of a Gantt chart, which is a format that some project managers use to organize their work. Employers, like people in foreign lands, are impressed and flattered when you speak to them in their own language.

Creative resumes are most appropriate for people applying to public relations, advertising, or marketing firms. (I wouldn't advise accountants, for instance, to design their resumes like spreadsheets.) If your work is portable—if, for instance, you're an architect and can carry pictures of your designs—it's a good idea to attach photographs or drawings to the resume. Videotaped resumes, which are becoming more common, might be useful for presenters, trainers, or theatrical performers.

FIVE BASES TO COVER IN YOUR COVER LETTER

Cover letters do matter. And the more precisely you can customize them to each employer, the better. (See sample cover letter on page 173.)

In discussing resumes with small-company presidents, I was surprised to find out just how strongly they feel about cover letters. They expect cover letters to:

- Be personally addressed to the president or appropriate member of the management team. To do that, look up the

Simple Rules for Effective Resume Writing

- **Be truthful.** Many small employers will check your references, and some even hire investigators to make sure the resume is factual. One engineer listed a fictitious MBA degree, even though his professional experience was so substantial that he didn't need one. He was found out and lost an excellent job as a result.

- **Be consistent.** Everything you say should reinforce your objective. Tailor each item so that it adds weight to your argument that you should be hired in the capacity you seek.

- **Customize the resume for each employer.** The more closely you adapt your resume to the needs and expectations of the employer, the better. As mentioned before, a computer or word processor can help you whip out a new resume in minutes. College libraries often have computer rooms where word processors are available for public use.

- **Eliminate typographical, spelling, or grammatical errors.** Remember that your resume may be the first example of your work that an employer sees. Use the spell checker on your word processor to screen for misspelled words. Ask a friend to proofread the resume for you.

- **Accentuate the positive.** Make your best assets most prominent. Some people err by starting each entry in their job history with the dates of their tenure. Dates have little importance. Lead each paragraph with your title or a description of your accomplishments.

- **Don't leave unexplained gaps in your history.** Few things alarm employers as much as an unexplained absence from the work force. They worry that you might have spent that time in a federal minimum-security prison. Anything is better than leaving the gap up to a reader's imagination.

- **Be concise.** Try to limit the resume to one page. Describe your responsibilities at previous jobs as briefly as possible. Use simple, direct language while avoiding clichés and overuse of the word *I*. To save space, eliminate your earliest jobs or summarize them.

company in a standard directory. If all else fails, call and ask the receptionist for the name you need. (One CEO tosses away any cover letter that's not personally addressed to him. "I don't want to see a 'Dear sir or madam,' " he adds. "They should take the trouble to look my name up in a directory." Nor does he care for gushy promises that the applicant's sole ambition since early childhood has been to work for his company.)

- Use an eye-catching lead that breaks the ice and personalizes the letter. Refer to an event where you met someone from the company or to an article about the company that you read.

- Demonstrate a more-than-average familiarity with the company, its products, and its objectives. The more knowledgeable you can appear, the better. That's where your library, data-base, and networking legwork will come in handy.

- Clearly portray what you have to offer the company. Be as specific as possible. For instance, point to your familiarity with a market that you know the company wants to enter.

- Do not state your salary requirement unless it has been specifically requested. If it has, put down a range and emphasize that you're willing to link compensation to performance.

In short, the cover letter presents a literary challenge. Like all good writing, it should sound spontaneous, even though it has been carefully thought out. It should convey enthusiasm—but not a trace of desperation. And it should give the impression that you know more about the company and its industry than the average person does.

If you've read an article about your target company, or if you've published an article that's pertinent to the company, attach it to your cover letter. It will make your resume stick out and it will impress the reader.

PRIME TARGETS FOR YOUR RESUME, IN ORDER OF IMPORTANCE

Now that your resume is all dressed up, where should it go? To any of the following:

- *Networking meetings and interviews.* Bring resumes along on any occasion where you would also bring business cards. Seventy percent of all job seekers find their jobs through networking.

- *Want ads.* About 15 percent of all small-company job seekers find their jobs through want ads. Small companies usually don't have human-resource departments, so they rely on want ads when networking fails.

- *Your target companies.* Mail unsolicited resumes to specific executives at your target companies. Mention in your cover letter that you will follow up with a phone call. Then call the executive either very early or very late in the day. Twelve percent of those who find jobs at small companies find them through direct-mail solicitations.

- *Executive-search firms.* Some jobseekers obtain a list of executive-search firms and send resumes to them. "Headhunters" usually ignore over-the-transom applications, unless it can help them conclude their current search. Only about 3 percent of those who find jobs in small companies do so through recruiters, while up to 15 percent of all those who find jobs in large companies use recruiters.

FOLLOW UP OR FORGET IT!

Always follow up your resume with a phone call or a letter. Magazine publishers routinely mail out a dozen reminders to get you to renew a subscription. If you're targeting a small company, you'll need the same persistence. One client of mine finally landed his ideal position as director of marketing after two years and 20 contacts with the same company. Bullfrogs respect tenacity.

Whenever you read an article in the press about one of the companies you've applied to, clip it out and send it to your interviewer, along with a thoughtful note. Use every excuse you can to follow up.

Sample Cover Letter

Janet Jeffries, President
Medicorp Inc.
1111 Alameda Blvd.
San Jacinto, CA 99999

Dear Ms. Jeffries,

At the Healthworld trade show last week I saw your presentation of the new XT diagnostic imaging equipment and software. I was very impressed with your product, your demonstration, and your company's entrepreneurial spirit. You might remember me. I was the one in the back asking the questions.

Though I currently own an active consulting firm, I'd like to "sink my teeth" into one solid company. I would like to explore the possibility of applying my eight years' experience in operating, planning, and marketing medical products in a growth-oriented company like MediCorp.

I have demonstrated my abilities through the following accomplishments:

- Developed a successful marketing campaign for multisite diagnostic imaging firm that garnered national publicity and produced a 20% increase in growth.
- Spearheaded a marketing effort for a nursing home that led to 15% annual growth in occupancy.
- Founded and managed a consulting practice with over 40 clients.

Do you need someone who can "plan and do" and consistently exceed expectations? I'd like to share my marketing ideas with you and discuss opportunities that might exist within MediCorp. I will call you next week to set up an appointment.

Sincerely,

attachment: resume or professional profile

Sample Resume

Jane Smith
123 Grantham St.,
Santa Barbara,
CA 99999
805-123-4567

Objective

Marketing Management position requiring strong analytic, operations, and business-development skills in the San Francisco Bay Area.

Summary Statement

A management professional with eleven years' experience, seven as a principal in the marketing or planning departments of large manufacturing companies and four years as a small-company turnaround expert in a management-consulting firm.

Selected Skills and Accomplishments

Marketing Management. Astute, customer-oriented market analyst with a focus on product development and financially successful marketing. Effective marketing-plan creator.

- Directed complete marketing effort to turn a stagnant manufacturer of construction products from a loss of 5% to a profit of 4% in three years with over 15% growth.
- Created a successful marketing program for a multisite diagnostic imaging and occupational health firm, achieving excellent publicity and a 20% growth increase.

Business Analysis. Resourceful, action-oriented analyst with a keen ability to focus on key issues, who thrives on variety and challenges. Grounded in financial results with strong communications skills.

- Instituted changes to improve communications, quality assurance, and employee satisfaction in a multidivisional service firm with growth in excess of 200% over two years.

- Facilitated the change to a customer orientation for a specialty chemical manufacturer.
- Revitalized a manufacturer in a mature market to achieve profitability and 50% growth.

Entrepreneurship. Hands-on innovative leader who brings new products and services to market. Identifies viable niches and methods to reach them. Able to translate ideas into direct action.

- Founded a local monthly publication with 30,000 circulation, which received national recognition and originated a trade show with over 50 exhibitors and 3,000 visitors.
- Developed a consulting practice with over 40 clients in diverse markets.
- Formulated a marketing campaign for nursing home that led to 15% annual increase in residents.

Experience

Principal, Global Consulting Inc., Los Angeles, CA	1988–1992
Adjunct Professor of Management, UC-Santa-Barbara, CA	1985–1989
Marketing Manager, U.S. Health Ventures, Santa Barbara, CA	1985–1988
Senior Business Strategist, AT&T, Parsippany, NJ	1983–1985
Systems Analyst, E. I. Du Pont de Nemours & Co., Wilmington, DE	1981–1982

Education

A.B., magna cum laude, The Undergraduate School, Wilmington, DE
Major in economics, minor in German

Business and Professional Affiliations

American Marketing Association	Board of Directors, Vice President
Forum of Executive Women	Cofounder (1992) and Chair of Organizing Committee
Small Business Development	Advisory Board and Expo Steering Committee

Swimming Lessons

Your resume is, in a sense, your ticket to a better life. As your job-search experience grows and your plans for the future evolve, you'll rewrite it many times. It is a living document. The very act of writing the resume can be a excellent exercise in self-examination. We often don't know what we know or believe until we force ourselves to put it on paper. Resumes are worth writing for that reason alone.

Don't underestimate the power of a cover letter. This simple, one-page letter should convey to the small-business person that you're an articulate and intelligent individual who understands the target company's needs. Present yourself as the kind of versatile, energetic, independent-minded person who thrives in a small-business environment.

Remember that your resume may well be the first impression that small-business executives have of you. It is the bait or the lure that grabs their attention. Not every kind of bait will attract every kind of fish, but when you put the right bait in front of the right fish, you'll get at least a nibble. You might even get a bite.

CHAPTER TWELVE

Facing the Bullfrog: The Small-Company Job Interview

The wisest words I've heard spoken about job interviews came from a young marketing director who had worked at a series of small software firms and knew exactly what small-company interviewers are waiting to hear.

"A small company," he says, "is interested in how you can help them solve their problems. If you can find out a lot about those problems before the interview and prepare for the interview as if it were a sales call, they will say to themselves, 'Great. Finally we've found somebody who thinks the way we do.'"

In a small-company interview the more you know about the company, the more the interviewer will take you seriously. Small-company interviews tend to be more personal and less standardized than interviews at large companies, where interviewers try to stick to a corporate-wide interviewing procedure. Such a policy would rarely exist at a small company.

As we pointed out in Chapter Four, small-company "bull-frogs" need answers to three basic questions: (a) Can you add value to the company? (b) Can you fit into the culture of a small company, with its demands for flexibility and versatility? and (c) Can you work more or less harmoniously with him (or her)? If you've checked into the bullfrog's background, the stage of his company, and the industry it's in, you'll be better able to answer those questions.

In this chapter we'll talk about several aspects of interviewing, including how to angle for an interview with a well-written query letter, how to develop a 60-second infomercial about yourself, how to negotiate compensation, and how to deliver what we call your positive blurt. We'll conclude with a note on the most important but most neglected aspect of the interview process: the follow-up.

Even when interviews don't lead directly to job offers (you'll rarely receive an offer on the spot anyway), interviews can help you learn more about your industry, bring new people into your network, and possibly help you win a consulting or free-lance assignment that might lead to a full-time job.

Remember that the object of a job interview is not necessarily to "get a job." The object is to find out whether you, the position, and the company are suitably matched. One entrepreneur who attended my focus group offered this advice to people embarking on job interviews: "Don't try to figure out what they want. Just figure out what you want." On the one hand, you must find out what your prospective employer wants and needs. But you shouldn't contort yourself to fit those needs. If you keep your own goals clearly in mind, interviewing can be a pleasure.

PREPARING FOR THE INTERVIEW

Getting invited to the party

One person, looking for a financial position, spotted an article about an interesting company in his local business tabloid. The company, which sold high-quality software to firms that market data management systems to airlines and hospitals, was laying off employees due to falling sales—as it had more than once in the past.

Like a bottom fisher who spots undervalued stocks, he saw opportunity for himself in the company's hard times. He dispatched a letter to the president saying that he was "tired of seeing another article" about his problems. He "knew what was wrong with the company and had some ideas on how to fix it." In just a few well-chosen words he had baited his hook with an offer too good to refuse. He was offered an interview immediately.

"They were impressed that I'd taken a stab at their problems and that I was enthusiastic about it," he says. His interview led to three free-lance marketing assignments, and finally to a full-time job with this small publicly held company.

The ideal way to secure an interview is through a friend within the company. Lacking that, you must find a way, as this person did, to wrangle an invitation. It's okay to be aggressive—most small-business people welcome that. One CEO says he encourages everyone who sends in a resume or calls him on the phone to visit if they're "in the neighborhood." If they visit—and only about one in ten ever does—he knows they've got moxie. As with most closed doors in life, it never hurts to knock.

Developing a 60-second infomercial

Every good salesperson does it. You need to do it too. Before you embark on an interview, develop a brief informal statement that conveys your essence in a minute or less. It should encapsulate what you can do and what you're looking for.

Start the way a newspaperman does: with a bright "lead" that captures your theme in one pithy sentence. You might say, "I specialize in bringing new products to market," or "I help small companies find the managers they need," or "I help small manufacturing firms cut their rework rates in half." In a dozen words or less, tell the interviewer exactly what sort of "hired gun" you are.

After that explain what management level you're interested in, what roles and functions you'd like to perform, and what kind of setting you're looking for. By "setting" we mean industry, stage of corporate development, geographical location, size of company, and so on. In this case, of course, you're looking for a small company.

Try to show how your skills, abilities, and preferences will fit the company's needs. At the end ask the interviewer what the company's activities or needs are in your area. You'll know whether you've hooked them by the interest they begin to show.

Dress as you'd like to be perceived

Not long ago I was interviewed by a British company that needed an American headhunter to help them fill a position at their U.S. subsidiary. The company's CEO, I learned by calling people in my network, was a stickler for good grooming. So I dry-cleaned my most formal business suit, had my blouse pressed, and carefully shined my shoes. If my interview had been with Bagel Works, a socially conscious baking company in Vermont, I might have dressed more down-to-earth. But dressing in conservative business attire never hurts. My two rules of thumb: Dress as you'd like to be perceived, and wear clothes that are one notch above what you can usually afford.

MAKE THE MOST OF THE INTERVIEW

Talking with the bullfrog

Small-company interviews come in all shapes and sizes. If you come highly touted by someone close to the CEO, for instance, you might get the job without a formal interview. On the other hand, the interview process may take months as you pass through a series of meetings. You might be interviewed by one person, by a team, or by a series of people.

Some small-company executives rely on seat-of-the-pants instincts to make a hiring decision. Those who have big-company backgrounds and those who've made hiring mistakes in the past may use a battery of tests and reference-checking services. Some small-firm CEOs interview dozens of candidates before making a decision to hire. Others interview only a handful. Some interviewers sit where they can observe your body language. Others remain behind their desks.

As we mentioned earlier, you can sometimes predict interviewing styles by a company's industry and stage of development, as well as by the president's background. But no two small-company interviews will be quite the same. That's part of what makes the small-company job search so stimulating.

Questions mother never told you they'd ask

Like Frank Sinatra, the CEOs of small companies like to do things "my way." In interviews they sometimes ask sly, whimsical, or provocative questions. While these questions might appear hostile, their intent is simply to help the interviewer fish for clues about your talents and character.

The best way to respond to these questions is to volunteer the personal information for which the interviewer is indirectly asking. The worst reaction would be to take the questions too literally, since that might lead you to become defensive and clam up. Doing so would frustrate the interviewer and make you seem hard to work with. Here are some unusual questions that small-company interviewers I know have asked:

• *"What were you like in high school?"* One vice president of a small biotech company firmly believes that people who have made a conscious change in their personality, behavior, or goals are better suited to a high-risk, entrepreneurial work environment. He's looking for the kind of person (not unlike himself) who wore dark sunglasses, smoked cigarettes, and played bass guitar in a rock band in high school, then got serious and pursued a master's in business or engineering.

- *"How would you balance the federal budget?"* The managing partner of a computer-consulting firm asks this question just to hear how you answer it. What he really wants to know is how flexible and quick-witted you are.

- *"Can you prove to me that you're flexible?"* Small-company CEOs are more likely to hire you if they believe that, even though you're a center fielder, you can play first and third base as well. The best answer is one that illustrates that you can "keep a lot of different plates spinning at the same time."

- *The intentional pregnant pause.* One president allows the conversation to grind to a halt, just to see whether the interviewee can take control of the situation or, better yet, turn the tension into laughter. If you can relieve the silence with humor, you'll have passed the test.

- *"If this were your company, what would you do with it?"* The president of a small boutique bank—one of the new banks that are springing up to fill the niches not filled by the big money-center banks—asks this question when he interviews prospective executives. Anyone who couldn't answer the question would be either underqualified for the job or unprepared for the interview.

- *"Sell this watch back to me!"* This is a statement, not a question. But one entrepreneur I know uses it during interviews to find out how good a salesman the candidate is likely to be.

- *"What are you goals?"* Your answer to this question will reveal your values and whether your values match the goals of the company. If you're applying for a sales job, the most compelling reply might be, "I want to drive a BMW and live in the best part of town." For a job in the high-tech start-up it might be, "I want to be on the cutting edge of technology." In a "green" company it may be, "I want to help society and preserve the earth." The best answer, of course, is the one that's true.

The "positive blurt"

One small-company president has said, "I'm impressed if people sound clearly like themselves. I need to feel that they've found that place inside themselves that makes their heart sing."

In other words, it's essential to be authentic in a job interview. A successful interview usually contains a moment of truth when either you break through and give the interviewer a vivid sense of yourself and your value or the moment passes and you leave without making a strong impression.

At the beginning of my workshops I ask everyone to describe themselves and the kind of work they're looking for. Most of them recite a dry list of previous employers, job titles, and degrees. They don't sound "clearly like themselves."

Later, at the end of the workshop, after we've become comfortable with each other, I repeat the process. This time I ask all of them to tell the others who they really are and what they do best.

That's when they begin to blossom. Some of them will suddenly come out with impressive, unselfconscious descriptions of themselves and their skills, in plain language and without mentioning either employers or titles. I call it the positive blurt. Their heart starts talking instead of their head. They exude charisma and honesty. They become real people rather than stick figures. And when they get the hang of doing this, it becomes easy. They don't have to rehearse or memorize it. It's who they really are.

It's not easy to know when to deliver the positive blurt. Picking the wrong time to make a passionate statement is a good way to make a fool of yourself. My advice would be to come out with your positive blurt (a) if the interviewer asks you to describe yourself; (b) if the interviewer's attention seems to be drifting; or (c) at the end of the interview in which you don't think you've really made a strong enough impression. Timing is everything. Use your instincts.

"Case the joint"

A job interview also gives you a chance to "case the joint." Sometimes you can tell a lot about a business just by checking to see how neat and clean they keep the kitchen area or bathroom.

Talk to as many people as you can meet, from the receptionist to the vice presidents.

One former Hewlett-Packard systems engineer and his spouse made a habit of taking prospective employers and their spouses out to dinner as an informal interview. He had used this technique when hiring people at H-P, and now he uses it when he's looking for a job. You can learn a lot about people, he says, by observing how considerate they are of their spouses.

Squeeze every drop out of the interview

Whether or not interviews lead to full-time job offers, they represent opportunities to network, publicize yourself, hone your job-search techniques, and refine your self-presentations. Use the interview to:

- *Add the interviewer to your network.* The person who interviews you undoubtedly knows many other executives in the field. He or she can give you valuable information about people and trends in the industry that will help your job search.

- *Talk your way into a consulting or free-lance assignment.* Short-term assignments often lead to full-time jobs. They give you and the employer a chance to get acquainted without the financial and contractual pressures that go along with a formal job offer.

- *Learn all you can about the industry.* A company might not give you a guided tour of their facilities if you were employed full-time at one of its competitors. But when you're looking for a job, you can walk the factory floor, ask probing questions, and see things you'd never otherwise see. Take advantage of this opportunity to absorb information.

- *Find out the full range of openings.* Open yourself to the possibility that you might fit into the company in a very different job than the one you first applied for. During interviews reveal all your skills and interests. The company may have *several* jobs that you're qualified for. You may not find out about them until you're interviewed.

- *Refine your interviewing style.* Ask the interviewer how

well you presented yourself and how you might present yourself more effectively. If you're shooting yourself in the foot somehow, ask for feedback on the problem and correct it. One person insisted on knowing why he wasn't offered a particular job, and when he discovered that he failed to project sufficient enthusiasm, he changed his behavior. Two months later he found a job.

OVERCOMING INTERVIEWER BIASES

A lot of job seekers worry about possible hidden prejudices or biases that interviewers might hold against them, or against something on their resume. Such biases exist, but don't let them discourage you. Instead, be aware of them and work to overcome them or to turn them into potential assets.

A weak point can be a strong point in disguise

As long as you're comfortable with who you are, you don't have to be afraid that an interviewer will unnerve you with questions about your "weak" points. Every so-called weak point is potentially a strong point in disguise. You're not old—you're more experienced. You're not too young—you're enthusiastic and unspoiled by bad habits. You're not undereducated—you're a self-made person.

If you're a member of a racial minority, emphasize your success in working with clients of every color and nationality or your ability to introduce the company to a new market. If you're older, show spunk and mention that you swim or play racquetball (only if you do of course). If you've only worked at large companies, mention that you worked in a family business early in your career, or helped out in your spouse's small business, or served as treasurer on the board of directors of an arts organization.

You don't have to be perfect to find a job. You just have to be capable. If your "weak point" doesn't bother you, it's less likely to bother anyone else.

How the "outplaced" can win small-business people over

As we'll point out elsewhere in this book, many small-business people hold certain biases against former large-company executives. "Most corporate executives know nothing about small business," says Fred Beste, a Pennsylvania-based venture capitalist. "Working in a small company is like working on a trapeze without a net. It's very hard for big-company managers to ratchet down their lifestyle to the demands of a small company."

Indeed, outplaced executives must either work hard to overcome such prejudice or find someone in their network who trusts their abilities. Joseph G. was able to do both.

Mr. G. had entered a giant computer-manufacturing firm immediately after graduating college. He worked there for 18 years and attained an $80,000-a-year position as controller of a division, where his principal role was ensuring that financial policies established by the executive committee were implemented by people at branch offices in the field. But he lost his job when the company downsized following a merger. His nearly two decades of loyal service, ironically, weren't enough to save his job, which was given to someone with *thirty* years of service.

Bloodied but unbowed (and buoyed by a decent severance package that included outplacement counseling), he sprang into his job search, applying all of his professional skills to the task. He built a computer data base of network contacts and cross-indexed them by name of person and name of company. He sent frequent letters and fliers to the people in his network so they wouldn't forget him, made hundreds of phone calls, and wrote draft after draft of his resume.

He waited months for results. Though often a finalist for jobs that attracted hundreds of applications, he learned that he was considered overqualified (that is, he was asking for too much money). Still he persevered and eventually found a high-paying CFO position through an old network contact, the owner of a $33 million family business who'd offered him a financial job seven years before. To overcome the prejudice against him, Mr. G.

finally had to find someone who already knew him and knew that he was worth every penny he was asking for.

Mr. G. was just one of hundreds of thousands of highly paid corporate executives who found themselves out of work in the wake of the so-called restructuring, downsizing, and right-sizing that have been corporate America's corrective to overexpansion and shrinking market share.

Small businesses need people like him for the first-class training and experience they've accumulated. Unfortunately many small-company CEOs, particularly those who have not worked in large corporations, worry that outplaced managers must have been deadwood in their old companies. It's an old story: People often assume that if something bad happens to you, you must have done something to deserve it.

Some of the outplaced people I've met take this harsh judgment to heart and blame themselves for the loss of their jobs. They tell themselves that they should have managed their careers more skillfully. Indeed, the emotional fallout from an involuntary layoff can be devastating.

One 53-year-old executive broke up with his wife after he lost his $200,000-a-year corporate job. She was embittered by the company's lack of gratitude for his 25 years of service and by the half-dozen relocations their family had endured. Her bitterness divided her from her husband and ruined—or helped ruin—their marriage. The most mature executives find a way not to take their layoffs personally. They bounce back pretty well and go right into their job search. These pragmatists have the best chance of finding new careers in small business.

Those who have been "outplaced" should present themselves as people who can succeed in the gritty world of small business. It all starts with a positive attitude. In my seminars I've seen two outplaced people sitting side by side who made extremely different impressions. One was taciturn and blank-faced—the very image of the defeated organization man. The other chatted amiably about his hands-on role as the treasurer of his wife's small business. He made it easy for others to forget that he was a corporate refugee and not a lifelong small-business person.

Skepticism toward outplaced workers, of course, is inversely proportional to the size of the company. As small businesses grow past 80 or 100 employees, they begin to resemble large companies—especially if the CEO or president was trained in a large corporation.

In any case the small-company CEO needs to be reassured that despite your years on the payroll of a large corporation, you have not grown soft or spoiled and can understand the small-company environment and thrive in it.

Small-business executives may have unrealistically high expectations of a former corporate executive. That's especially true if the small-business person is paying him or her a very high salary. In one instance, a 57-year-old former insurance executive was hired as COO by a 63-year-old small-business owner at a salary of $100,000—more than the entrepreneur had ever paid an employee. When the owner casually mentioned that he wanted four business and marketing plans written in the first six months, the executive assumed he was exaggerating. The owner wasn't, and the two men parted company after nine months.

There are two lessons here: First, former executives should recognize that small employers often expect near-miracles from highly paid newcomers; second, never assume that the interviewer is exaggerating when he tells you what he expects.

MBAs: their high expectations worry small-business people

The MBA degree from a good business school has come to be regarded as a ticket to success in American business—and perhaps a prerequisite, along with a finance and law degree, for success at the highest levels.

But what would be an advantage in a big-company search might be a disadvantage in a small-company search. MBAs should know that some small-business people blame MBAs and their ivory-tower theories for much of what's wrong with big business in America.

A small-company CEO might also worry that the MBA will

expect too much money, ask for a clearly defined career path, and want to spend more time on strategic planning than on the mundane, real-life questions such as, "How are we going to cover our expenses?"

"MBAs don't want to take a subordinate job," says the vice president of marketing of a medical-products company, who happens to have an MBA from Harvard and likes to hire MBAs as long as they've got their feet on the ground. "They want to be in on the decision-making right from the start."

Many MBAs, he adds, are high-achievers who get ahead by learning the "rules of the game" when they join a new school or organization and then try to move up the ladder by playing the game better than anybody else.

But in small business the rules may change from day to day, and anyone who relies on predictability might become confused and frustrated. "We want somebody who looks beyond the immediacy of the game," this vice president says.

Paradoxically, he says, he's looking for someone who can handle a lot of responsibility but who doesn't try to grab it until it's offered. In other words, he needs confident decision makers, but he doesn't like new people who elbow their way into the decision-making process whether they can contribute or not.

If you're an MBA interviewing at a small company, remember that the interviewer may assume that you're too theoretical, too ambitious, and too rule-oriented to be happy working for him. To offset that prejudice, make sure that you mention, for instance, your love of entrepreneurship, any hands-on experience you might have gained during a semester of work-study, and your lack of concern for titles.

FOLLOWING UP

Keep your name fresh in the minds of the people who interview you. That means reminding them that you're still interested in the job and awaiting their decision. You can do this in several ways:

- *The thank-you note.* After the interview, write a thank-you letter that reminds the interviewer what you talked about and includes new information that answers questions you might have left hanging.
- *The telephone call.* It's fine to telephone the interviewer, but give him or her fair warning about when you'll call. At the end of the in-person interview, or in the thank-you letter, suggest a time when you'll call back. If they liked you, they won't mind hearing from you.
- *Faxes.* If time is short, send a fax. Faxes are no longer a novelty, they're just another communication tool. Sending a fax can show that you're electronically up-to-date.

Creative follow-ups

For those in professional consulting, sales, marketing, advertising, or public relations, a creative follow-up can impress a company with your enthusiasm, imagination, and determination.

A cake and The New York Times. For instance, one recent graduate with a degree in marketing applied for an ad agency job. He was too young and inexperienced, however, and he wasn't called back for a second interview.

Instead of giving up, he sent the company a cheeky reminder written in icing on a layer cake made by his father-in-law, a baker. The company invited him back for another interview, but still didn't offer him the job.

Then he placed a classified ad in *The New York Times* that said, in effect, "To Bob and Mary. Look No Farther. You interviewed the best candidate at 4 P.M. last Thursday." To make sure the agency people didn't miss the ad, he asked his wife to call their office with an anonymous tip.

He didn't get the job. But he probably would have had the company not been purchased and downsized a few months later. He went on to start his own $1.5 million market-research firm.

A rose is a rose is a . . . full-time job. One woman, applying for a job at a small consulting firm that installs LANs, or local area network systems, sent the company one rose each week for six weeks after her interview, along with a note that read, "You're really missing the boat by not hiring me." Eventually she was hired.

If you follow up, you'll be doing more than 80 percent of all job seekers do. If you use a creative follow-up, you'll be doing more than 99 percent.

HOW TO HAGGLE CREATIVELY FOR YOUR COMPENSATION

Assuming that a small company offers you a job, you'll soon reach the salary-negotiation stage. As the walrus in Lewis Carroll's "Jabberwocky" put it, 'The time has come to talk of cabbages . . .' In other words, cash.

Negotiating a salary at a small company involves much more improvisation than at a large company, where there are time-honored, carved-in-granite traditions (or so they might want you to believe) about compensation. Small companies are less likely to have fixed policies. You can customize a compensation package much more easily.

Sometimes you must even help the small company find a way to afford you. If a small company can't pay you what you want, create a blend of perks, bonuses, commissions, and base pay that will provide you with a level of compensation that satisfies you and enables the company to squeeze you in under its salary cap. Agents for major-league athletes do this routinely.

Stock options, a company car or mileage reimbursement, parking privileges, a sign-on bonus, or extra paid vacation days are just some of the forms of compensation you can take instead of salary. Others include payment of tuition for continuing education, compensation of spouses for paperwork performed at home, flexible work hours, freedom to work at home, generous sales commissions and bonuses, or paid moving expenses. If your spouse can cover you with his or her health insurance, you can even forgo health benefits in return for cash.

Be creative. Consider your needs and the company's needs. Are they starving for new customers? They might pay you very high sales commissions and bonuses. Do you have enormous college tuition bills? Perhaps they can loan you money at a low rate. Do you like to ski? Maybe the company owns a time-share in Vail or Stowe that you can use. Ask questions. Find out.

Don't let a great opportunity slip away by taking a hard line on base salary. One $80,000-a-year corporate executive who had lost his job was interviewing for a job he really wanted at a small company. The company, however, would only offer a $60,000 base salary to start, but could offer equity that would boost him up to $90,000 on paper. He got insulted, however, and walked away without exploring alternate forms of compensation. He now has a routine job with no equity and is kicking himself.

Another job seeker, a former $200,000-a-year executive in his mid-50s who was turned out of his chemical-corporation job during a restructuring, recommends three numbers to keep in mind when trying to arrive at a satisfactory salary figure with a small-company CEO. "You have to consider the amount that you know you're worth," he says, "the amount you're worth to that employer, and the amount that that employer can afford to pay. Those three numbers can either be far apart or close together."

He knew he was worth $200,000, but he believed the company could only afford $100,000. He finally got $90,000—an amount equal to the president's salary. To balance the package, he negotiated for flexible hours and more vacation.

Remember that everything is negotiable. And if you can convince the company that you will make it more profitable, you'll be in a much stronger position to negotiate. The idea of matching "pay for performance" is currently in vogue at large companies. It has never been out of vogue at small companies.

Swimming Lessons

Interviews are the fruit of your search and networking efforts. They represent more than just an opportunity to obtain a full-time job. You can use an interview to find out more about an industry, to offer your services as a consultant, or to extend your network in a new direction. It never hurts to tack another executive's name to your list of industry contacts.

Prepare carefully for the interview by reading or asking friends about the company and its executives. Give the interviewer a sense of who you really are, what you do best, and how your skills might improve the company's bottom line. When discussing compensation, help the company find a way to afford you. Remember, too, that the object of the interview isn't just to get a job but to determine whether you and the company will make a suitable and compatible match.

Tips

- Remember what the bullfrog wants. Emphasize how you can add to the value of the business, what you know about the company, and search for common ground between you and your prospective boss.
- Don't be shy about taking the initiative and asking for an interview even when no opening has been advertised. The CEO may not know she needs you until she meets you, and if she has the clout she may hire you on the spot.
- Do your due diligence. Investigate the company thoroughly before, during, and after your interview. Call everyone who knows the company. On your interview ask everyone you meet about the company. Check on the cleanliness of the kitchen and bathrooms.
- If the company can't meet your salary demands but you still want the job, brainstorm to create a blend of perks, bonuses, vacation days, and health benefits that will satisfy your needs.
- Use a word processor and printer to pump out professional-looking correspondence that can be easily customized and updated. If you don't already own a computer, a printer, and a modem, it might be wise to invest in them. But be wary of cheap computer printers that produce terrible-looking documents. And resist the temptation to gussy up your letters with all those fancy typefaces that the word processor puts at your disposal.

- Don't talk too much! More than once my corporate clients have rejected otherwise qualified job seekers who simply don't know when to stop talking. Yes, you need to be forthcoming and communicative. But people who babble on, either because they are nervous or just naturally loquacious, make a poor impression during interviews. It's simply bad manners. The same holds true for written correspondence. Don't send a nine-page follow-up letter when a one-page note will do.

CHAPTER THIRTEEN

Digging Your Own Pond: How Four Big-Company Professionals Started Businesses of Their Own

Many people have carried the concept of making a big splash in a small pond to its logical conclusion by digging ponds of their own. Millions of Americans, in fact, start small businesses every year. Quite a few of them are former corporate executives who have put away enough savings, accumulated enough savvy, and recognized that they have little to lose and much to gain by going into business for themselves.

In the course of researching this book I talked to several former executives and professionals who started their own small companies after getting ousted from large corporations. One cobbled a business together with his own "sweat equity." Another purchased a franchise and opened a storefront business. A third became a consultant specializing in bringing new products to market. And a fourth started a tiny manufacturing firm.

I'd like to tell the stories of four of these people. My purpose isn't to glorify the act of starting a small business or to offer advice on how to do so. I simply feel that reading about the experiences of four outplaced workers who have started their own companies can be instructive to just about anyone who has been turned out of a big company and wants to explore the small-business job market.

Why? Because the skills needed to start a small business—versatility, resourcefulness, tenacity and so forth—are the same skills needed to work effectively in small business. Similarly the "attitude" needed to start a small business—an ability to present yourself as a partner who offers money-making ideas rather than a mere employee who asks for handouts—is the same attitude you'll need to convince a CEO that you're suited to small business. People who start businesses aren't very different from other job seekers. They've merely taken that last evolutionary step and turned into bullfrogs.

At the same time, I believe that hearing about the triumphs and trials of other former managers can boost the morale of anyone who has experienced an involuntary early retirement or outplacement. Hundreds of thousands of Americans have gone quietly through this unwelcome rite of passage in recent years. Many of them blame themselves unnecessarily for events far beyond their control. Knowing that they aren't alone can only do them good.

COBBLING TOGETHER A BUSINESS OUT OF SPARE PARTS

Scott J., a 35-year-old computer scientist and mathematician, was one of the "lucky" ones who didn't lose his job when his employer, a giant computer manufacturer, began dismissing hundreds of employees. Unlike many of his colleagues, he was spared the indignity of being escorted from the building by security guards with the contents of his desk in a cardboard box.

But he wasn't really so lucky. As one of the survivors of the cuts, he was forced to help pick up the slack left by the people who were gone. At one point he was covering for so many people that he was billing his time to 13 separate project accounts.

Wanted control of own destiny. When he was asked to accept a transfer (a move that would have cost his wife her job), he quit his $60,000-a-year position and explored the idea of starting a small company of his own. "I was tired of being bounced around, and I wanted to be in control of my own destiny," he says. "I didn't have any money to start or buy a business, but I wanted the feel of being at least the part-owner of something."

To do that, Scott found a way to cobble together a new business out of spare parts. He spoke to a group of engineers at GE who were aware of several government research contracts that GE wasn't pursuing. Then he approached a healthy small company that specialized in the same sort of contracts. He proposed that the president give him enough money to start what would become a partially owned subsidiary. He would hire the GE engineers to moonlight on the projects that GE had chosen not to do.

A cash cow walking in off the street. "I found a small, privately owned company with a cash flow and a strong credit history, wrote up a business plan, and said to them, 'Let me have the profit-and-loss responsibility for a new spin-off profit center. I'll hire the engineers, get the contracts, and if the venture makes money, we'll both take some out.'

"A lot of people out there don't realize you can do that," Scott says. "To the company we represented a cash cow walking in off the street."

Having started that company, Scott looked for a new challenge. A friend knew of a Texas high-tech firm that owned a data-base technology it wasn't using. He and a partner created a company that would gather newly published scientific literature from government labs, universities, and technology-transfer firms, put it in a data base, and market it on-line to hundreds of companies hoping to commercialize new technologies.

The Texas company contributed its hardware and software,

plus start-up funds, in return for 50 percent ownership of the company. Another financial angel kicked in 25 percent. Scott provided the balance in the form of "sweat equity." Labs and universities were glad to provide their research findings in exchange for the free exposure to potential investors or licensees. Scott wrote the business plans, set up a five-person office, and started looking for customers.

Love of labor, not labor of love. Two years later his company is "close to profitability" and he's earning about $50,000. But his equity share could be worth millions.

Was life a little easier when he worked for a giant company? Yes, he'd say. Even though he was well suited to be a bullfrog—he had technical and business experience, and his wife had an excellent job—running a small company has been stressful.

"I would never recommend that you start a business just to get control over your time," he says. "Don't do it unless you think that the profits will outweigh the risks. Ninety-nine percent of all American workers say they'd like to run their own business. But most of them make the mistake of writing business plans that don't demonstrate to the investors where the profit is going to come from."

Offering rather than asking. Job seekers could make themselves much more attractive, he says, if they approached potential employers or partners with ideas for money-making ventures rather than simply requesting a job.

"If you walk into a company and ask for a job, they're not likely to give you the kind of profit-and-loss responsibility you're looking for," he says. "The trick is to go in proposing a partnership. When they hear 'partnership,' they think fifty–fifty. Instead of asking for something, you're offering something."

GOING THE FRANCHISE ROUTE

Allen M. had never planned to become the owner of a print-shop franchise. Then again, he never thought he'd lose his $110,000-a-year job as general manager of a Chicago-based subsidiary of a European chemical company. But after the parent company merged with a smaller competitor, Allen's entire division was eliminated.

As it happened, Allen was laid off on the same day he received a performance award from his company. At 10 A.M. one bright weekday he found himself being told by a vice president that he was no longer needed. Two hours later he appeared at a luncheon to accept a brass plaque for having turned his money-losing subsidiary into a profit center in only two years.

After the luncheon he climbed into the backseat of a company limousine, opened the liquor cabinet, and "drank a double Scotch. And then another double Scotch." Then he looked at the bright side. Eighteen months earlier the company had forced him and his wife to sell their beloved home in New Jersey and transfer to Chicago. Now they could move back.

"We can do anything we want." In fact Allen had good reason to feel optimistic. He was only 41. He had an MBA from a prestigious school. His work record was virtually spotless. And having gotten a year's salary as severance pay, he expected to take a long vacation and then ease into another general manager's job. "When we got the severance package," his wife, Kate, said, "our first thought was, 'We can do anything we want.' " They even talked about opening a small hotel or inn in a New England ski town.

But finding a new job wasn't easy, and after nine fruitless months of searching for a job with the help of an outplacement firm, Allen clipped an ad from *The Wall Street Journal* that said, "Golden Parachutes Land Here." It had been placed by a company that was selling franchises for quick-print shops based on Macintosh computers. Soon he found himself in a training camp with other former executives like himself, learning how to run a computer-based print shop. He paid $40,000 for the franchise and borrowed $250,000 for printing and copying equipment.

With his wife as unpaid partner, Allen opened a shop on a busy street corner in a small city in the Northeast that was enjoying a late-1980s boom. Overall the two were well suited for their new profession. They didn't mind the gritty hands-on work that running a print shop entails. "When I was in college," says Kate, "I had a job in a notebook bindery, so I don't mind the hands-on stuff such as cutting paper and stapling documents together."

Not unlike a mom-and-pop business. Still, it hasn't been easy. "Sales have steadily gone up, but after eighteen months we're not even where we thought we'd be in six months," he says. They work long hours, often choosing to substitute their own labor rather than pay out-of-pocket for hired help. They're at the mercy of the local economy and have difficulty finding reliable employees.

In short, they've discovered what it's like to run a traditional mom-and-pop business. "Sometimes my wife and I are up at three A.M., knocking our heads together and wondering why we ever did this," Allen says. "And then other days we're fine about it. If we didn't want to do this, we wouldn't be here."

Piecing several part-time consulting jobs into a full-time job

Better than anything else, Beverly T. liked to discover new technologies and come up with profitable commercial applications for them. Since being outplaced from a large textile company two years ago, she's built a consulting business around doing just that.

Beverly had always worked in large companies. She started her career at a chemical conglomerate, then transferred to a large medical-supply company, where she helped launch several successful products. But when she clashed with the company over long-term strategy—she wanted to take advantage of the growing market for large-diameter artificial blood vessels, while the company wanted to focus on small-diameter vessels—she started looking for new opportunities in small business.

Making sure the financial resources were there. She sent letters to 150 manufacturing companies in Delaware, offering her services as a commercialization consultant. Of the five responses she received, she focused on a start-up that hoped to market an electronic homing beacon, worn like a badge or a beeper, that would enable hospitals to track the movements of doctors and nurses.

To make sure the company was financially healthy, she got permission to study its books. She drafted a business plan and was offered a three-month assignment as a management consultant. The three months turned into four, and then five. She was told that if orders began flowing steadily, she'd be hired full-time.

In the meantime she has pieced together a full-time profession out of several part-time consulting assignments. She combs trade shows for leads on new companies and new technologies and is now helping an inventor commercialize a new type of water-aerating device for fish farmers.

"I like being able to look at a lot of different opportunities at the same time," she says. "I'm not stuck with one company. What I bring to the party is an ability to get the funding in the right place at the right time. But you don't just fall into these things. You have to have a clear idea of what you want to do."

THE CHALLENGE OF STARTING A SMALL MANUFACTURING FIRM

When he was given early retirement from a large chemical company in Delaware, Hugh R. was only 59 years old—one year short of qualifying for a full pension. The company had reversed its policy of holding on to experienced people and was rapidly replacing high-priced 30-year veterans like Hugh with younger managers earning 40 to 50 percent less.

Instead of retiring, Hugh, a graduate of MIT and the Harvard Business School, decided to start a small manufacturing firm. "In 1989 the economy was still booming, and I thought that I'd start a little company, provide employment to a few people, and give something back to the community. The incentive wasn't monetary. I was a little naive."

More obstacles than expected. Back in 1981 Hugh's former employer had discovered that thin sheets of the polypropylene film it was manufacturing could store a static-electric charge. As a result the film could cling to flat surfaces without adhesive, the way a rubber balloon sticks to a wall after you rub it on your hair. The company had no interest in commercializing this property, so Hugh used it to create an erasable, self-adhering writing surface that could replace traditional classroom chalkboards and easel pads.

Manufacturing the product was simple; one worker could produce 20 of the electrostatic sketch pads in an hour, or $75,000 worth of potential sales in a single week. But obtaining financing, setting up distribution channels, and achieving clear title to his idea, Hugh found, would be more problematic.

"Getting financing was an eye opener," he says. "I had read most of the popular journals and *Inc.* magazine. But when I went to the banks, I found that they will only loan you money if the loan is secured by your home." He approached a state-sponsored economic development office, which helped entrepreneurs by matching up to 25 percent or $75,000, of the amount they could borrow from their banks. Hugh won an initial loan, but his second installment was rejected because another entrepreneurial firm had defaulted the day before and the board of directors were suddenly more cautious.

Originally he hoped to market his product through office-supply stores. But as he laid out his first marketing plans, the office-supply business underwent an unprecedented shakeout. In 1989, 12,000 office-products dealers operated in the United States; the so-called super stores, such as Staples and Office Max, had only a 0.5 percent share of the market. By 1992 half of all the independent dealers had shut down, and the super stores had cornered 15 percent of the trade.

"That threw my original plans into a cocked hat," he says. "All of the industry studies I bought were useless." He knew that the super stores would dictate pricing and volume in ways that, as a tiny supplier, he would have difficulty complying with.

Then Hugh encountered an unexpected competitor. After exhibiting his product at a trade show in 1991, he received a threatening letter from attorneys for a $2.5 billion conglomerate. The conglomerate had obtained a patent on Hugh's product, claiming that it had invented the technology in 1986—a full five years after Hugh's former company stumbled across it. "Most people don't realize that the U.S. Patent Office issues patents without investigating the claim," Hugh says. His attorney called the conglomerate's bluff, and the larger company backed down. But Hugh still faced a deep-pocketed competitor.

Not for the average career executive. Still, Hugh, who has two children in college, doesn't regret his decision to start a small company. "We're still struggling to break even, but, personally, I'm much happier. I wish I'd left to start my own business twenty years ago. My father owned a small company, and I'd always had this interest. It's a wonderful feeling to be your own boss. There are a lot of thrills along the way."

But he wouldn't recommend this route for the average outplaced executive. "Most corporate types would not be suited to start a manufacturing business. I've always enjoyed making things. And I had a very unusual corporate career. Over my twenty-nine years I worked in marketing, operations, R and D, and finance. Few corporate executives have had that kind of broad training.

"You have to be a risk taker. Nothing happens in a small entrepreneurial company unless you do it yourself. I have to run the balance sheet and keep all the tax records. Middle and upper-level managers at big companies are just not used to that. I still miss my old colleagues. But none of my friends who still work for the corporation are happy. Most of them would leave in an instant if they had something better to go to."

Swimming Lessons

At first the experiences of these four self-made bullfrogs might seem irrelevant to someone who is simply looking for a job in a smaller company. On the contrary. The paths they followed, the skills and abilities they used, and the mental attitude they relied on are identical to the tools that any job seeker in the small-company market needs.

Like other job seekers, they *managed their job search like a*

What Four Outplaced Executives Learned About Starting Businesses

- *Don't reinvent the wheel.* You don't have to be a Thomas Edison to found a new business. Lots of unexploited ideas are sitting on the shelf somewhere waiting to be commercialized. Your old employer might even let you use one for a minimal fee.

- *Find a partner, not a banker.* Take your money-making ideas to an existing, well-run company in the same field and ask them to bankroll you or supply you with equipment or technology in return for a piece of your profits. If you have no cash of your own, put up "sweat equity."

- *Not everyone can be an executive.* Former corporate executives who have had broad experience in technology, finance, and management have the best chance of becoming successful entrepreneurs. Those whose children aren't in college, whose spouses work, and whose houses are paid for also have a better chance of weathering a small company's lean years.

- *Make it a love of labor, not a labor of love.* Those who try to turn a hobby into a business quickly find that the business leaves them no time for the hobby. You'll be more likely to succeed if you recognize that starting a small business means long hours, lower pay in the short run, and doing things—marketing, budgeting—that you may never have done before.

---

small business. They created business plans and sought out partners who needed their talents. Notice that none of them actually started a business from scratch. They positioned themselves as profit-centers, not as employees. That's how every job seeker in the small-company market must position him or herself.

They discovered how it feels to move suddenly from a big company to a small one. Instead of having assistants to handle trivial matters and policies to guide their decisions, they had to type their own letters and take responsibility for their actions. Anyone who enters the small-company marketplace for the first time has to make a similar adjustment.

Their search for new employment was, as it is for all job seekers, a journey of self-examination and self-discovery. Allen

M. and his wife learned to work side by side every day. Hugh R. fulfilled his desire to contribute something to his community. Scott J. exercised his entrepreneurial instincts in ways he couldn't have at Boeing or General Electric. Beverly T. specialized in what she loved to do: commercialize new technologies.

Finally, they demonstrated that it's possible not only to become a bigger fish in a smaller pond but to become the bullfrog. These four former executives didn't possess any superhuman qualities that other job seekers don't have. By starting companies, they simply carried their small-business job search to its logical conclusion.

Tips

- If you start a business, do it in a field that you already know something about. Scott J. knew the paper and chemicals business before he bought a printing franchise. Hugh R. knew a lot about the properties of plastic film before starting his manufacturing firm.
- Don't start a business unless you can prove to yourself and your investors that you actually have a good chance of making money. Don't idealize self-employment for its own sake.
- Recognize that when you go into business for yourself, you're actually taking on two jobs at once. The first job is delivering a specific product or service to your customers. The second job is running the business.
- Before your start a business, study your cash flow. People whose spouses have good jobs, whose mortgages are paid off, and who don't have college tuition expenses are the best candidates for starting small businesses. Those with big monthly bills to pay may not have the time to wait for a new venture to pay off.

Manage Your Job Search Like a Small Business, Revisited

I'd like to leave you with one thought above all others: *A job seeker must manage his or her job search as though it were a small business.* In other words, you must learn to think of yourself as a product, learn to think of small-business owners as your market, and learn to focus your strategies on penetrating that market. You must set aside ample time for self-analysis, for market research, and for identifying the most efficient marketing techniques for making small businesses aware of you.

If you take those steps, you'll be doing what every smart business in America does. But if you take those steps and also *perform all of the legwork yourself*—from replacing toner in your printer to logging every telephone call you make—then you'll be managing your job search as though it were a small business. By the end of your search you will not only have found a job in small business, you will know what it feels like to be a jack-of-all-trades manager in a small business.

At the same time, remember to customize the more traditional job-search techniques to suit the small-company job market. Aim your networking efforts at the small-business community. Learn to speak the language of small-business "bullfrogs," and use it when you meet them in interviews or when you write a resume, cover letter, or follow-up letter. Demonstrate that you appreciate the differences between large and small business and explain why a small company should hire you.

There's an ancient proverb that says, "If you serve someone a platter of fish, you feed him for a day. But if you teach him how to fish, you feed him for a lifetime." Forecasts indicate that we will need to fish for jobs more frequently in the coming decades. Most of us will switch jobs several times. Our only security will be our portfolio of transferable skills and experiences, and our ability to locate the right job in an increasingly turbulent labor market. Knowing how to look for a job will become an indispensable tool in the future.

A job search can also serve a higher purpose. Like any crisis, the crisis that precipitates a job hunt offers an opportunity for personal growth. I believe that during your search, you will become aware of skills, abilities, and preferences that you never knew you had. You will also learn to reach out to other people by creating or expanding your network. In the process you will grow. Your next job may or may not be the "perfect" job, if such a thing exists. But as you grow, you'll come closer to the ideal job.

Finally, I believe that dynamic small companies offer an exciting source of opportunity for hundreds of thousands of people like you. As large companies continue to downsize during the 1990s, virtually all the net job creation will occur in businesses with fewer than 100 employees. In the process, small companies will create opportunities for advancement, for freedom of expression in the workplace, and for a greater sense of accomplishment at the end of the workday. Finding the right small-business opportunity won't necessarily be easy. But this book, I'm certain, can help you reach it.

Bibliography

Adizes, Ichak. 1988. *Corporate Lifecycles: How and Why Corporations Grow and Die and What to Do About It.* Englewood Cliffs, NJ: Prentice-Hall.

Bardwick, Judith. 1986. *The Plateauing Trap: How to Avoid It in Your Career . . . and Your Life.* New York: American Management Association.

Barringer, Felicity. "Laid Off Bosses Scramble in a Changing World." *New York Times,* 12 July 1992, sec. E, p. 6.

Barron, James, and Alison Leigh Cowan, "Executives the Economy Left Behind." *New York Times,* 22 November 1992, sec. 3, p. 1.

Birch, David L. 1987. *Job Creation in America: How Our Smallest Companies Put the Most People to Work.* New York: The Free Press.

Brown, Charles; James Hamilton; and James Medoff. 1990. *Employers Large and Small.* Cambridge, MA: Harvard University Press.

Burton, Mary L., and Richard A. Wedemeyer. 1991. *In Transition: From the Harvard Business School Club of New York's Career Management Seminar.* New York: HarperBusiness.

Carey, Nancy B. 1992. "Breaking the Glass Slipper: Business Women's Style of Leadership." Unpublished thesis, Wharton School of Business, University of Pennsylvania.

Case, John. 1992. *From the Ground Up: The Resurgence of American Entrepreneurship.* New York: Simon & Schuster.

Drucker, Peter. 1989. *The New Realities: in Government and Politics, in Economic and Business, in Society and World View.* New York: Harper & Row.

Dunkelberg, William C.; Arnold C. Cooper; William J. Dennis, Jr.; and Carolyn Y. Woo. 1990. *New Business in America: The Firms and their Owners.* Washington, DC: The NFIB Foundation.

Ettorre, Barbara. "They're Not in the Army Now." *HR Focus.* January 1993, p. 22. New York: The American Management Association.

"For New Jobs, Help Small Business." *Wall Street Journal,* 10 August 1992.

Gerber, Michael E. 1986. *The E Myth: Why Most Businesses Don't Work and What to Do About It.* Cambridge, MA: Ballinger Publishing.

Hawken, Paul. 1983. *The Next Economy.* New York: Holt, Rinehart & Winston.

Hopkins, Kevin P., and William B. Johnston. 1988. *Opportunity 2000, Creative Affirmative Action Strategies for a Changing Workforce.* Indianapolis: Hudson Institute.

Kirchhoff, Bruce A., and Bruce D. Phillips. "Employment Growth in the Decade of the Entrepreneur." Lecture delivered at Babson College–University of Pittsburgh Entrepreneurship Research Conference, Pittsburgh, PA, 18 April 1991.

Koretz, Gene. "The White-Collar Jobless Could Really Rock the Vote." *Business Week,* 28 September 1992, p. 16.

Lacey, Dan. 1988. *The Paycheck Disruption: Finding Success in the Workplace of the '90s.* New York: Hippocrene.

Leinberger, Paul, and Bruce Tucker. 1991. *The New Individualists: The Generation After the Organization Man.* New York: HarperCollins.

Lewis, Michael. 1989. *Liar's Poker: Rising Through the Wreckage on Wall Street.* New York: Norton.

Lohr, Steve. "Big Companies Cloud Recovery by Cutting Jobs." *New York Times,* 17 December 1992, sec. A. p. 1.

Lohr, Steve. "Signs of Thaw for Small Business." *New York Times,* 4 November 1992, sec. D, p. 1.

Loscocco, Karyn A., and Joyce Robinson. "Barriers to Women's Small-Business Success in the United States." *Gender & Society,* v. 5, n. 4, December 1991, p. 511 ff.

Nasar, Sylvia. "Employment in Service Industry, Engine for Boom of 80's, Falters." *New York Times,* 2 January 1992, sec. A, p. 1.

Phillips, Bruce D. "The Increasing Role of Small Firms in the High-Technology Sector: Evidence from the 1980s." *Business Economics,* January 1991, p. 40 ff.

Phillips, Bruce D.; Bruce A. Kirchhoff; and H. Shelton Brown. "Formation, Growth and Mobility of Technology Based Firms in the U.S. Economy." 1990. U.S. Small Business Administration.

Reich, Robert B. 1991. *The Work of Nations.* New York: Alfred A. Knopf.

RoAne, Susan. 1988. *How to Work a Room.* New York: Warner Books.

Rosener, Judy B. "Ways Women Lead." *Harvard Business Review,* November–December 1990, pp. 119–25.

Small Business Economic Indicators: January–December 1991. July 1992. Washington, DC: Office of Advocacy, Small Business Administration.

Solomon, Steven. 1986. *Small Business USA: The Role of Small Companies in Sparking America's Economic Transformation.* New York: Crown.

Uchitelle, Louis. "America Isn't Creating Enough Jobs, And No One Seems to Know Why." *New York Times,* 6 September 1992, sec. 4, p. 1.

Uchitelle, Louis. "The Mothball Era in Arms Industry." *New York Times,* 22 September 1992, sec. D, p. 2.

U.S. Small Business Administration, Office of Advocacy. *The State of Small*

Business: A Report of the President. 1992. Washington, DC: U.S. Government Printing Office.

Wolfe, Tom. 1987. *The Bonfire of the Vanities.* New York: Farrar, Straus & Giroux.

"Women-Owned Businesses: The New Economic Force." 1992. Washington, DC: National Foundation for Women Business Owners.

Index

Adizes, Ichak, 49
adolescence, as a stage of a company's growth, 51
American Red Cross, The, 43
Apple Computer, 27
ARA Services, 116

Bagel Works Inc., 45, 75
Bardwick, Judith, 20
Ben & Jerry's Homemade Inc., 41, 45
Bertheide, Catherine White, Ph.D., 83
Beste, Fred, 116, 186
Bethlehem Steel, 25
"Big Six" accounting firms, 88, 128
Birch, David L., 26, 29, 68
Bonfire of the Vanities, 142

Brown, Charles, 29
Bryn Mawr College, 115
bullfrog (owner or CEO of small company):
  becoming a, 195–205
  expectations of, as revealed in focus groups, 92–98
  expectations of outplaced executives by, 188
  female of the species, 80–91
  minority, 76–77
  relationship with, 60–61
  three questions asked most often by, 68–77
  types of, 66–68, (chart), 70
Bureau of Labor Statistics, 47

Burpee, David, 130
Burpee Seed Company, W. Atlee,
    130
business services companies, 41

Campbell's Soup, 44
Capital Rose Inc., 83
Case, John, 26
Celestial Seasonings, 41
Census of Service Industries, 41
Center for Applied Research, Inc.,
    44
Challenger, Gray & Christmas, 128
Chrysler, 25
Clinton administration, 26
Cognetics, Inc., 27
Cold War, end of, 21
compensation:
    alternative forms of, 192
    at international companies, 40
    negotiating, 191–192
    at small companies, 39, 43, 48,
        56–57
Conner Inc., 47
Conte, Lisa, 87
Coopers and Lybrand, 47
courtship, as a corporate growth
    stage, 49–50
cover letters, 161, 169–171
    sample, 173

decision-making, at small compa-
    nies, 60
Department of Labor, U.S., 20, 82
director of marketing and sales, du-
    ties of in large and small com-
    panies, 102–104
Drozdow, Nancy, 44–45
Du Pont, 20, 28, 47, 60
due diligence, 34
    when evaluating a company, 193
Dunkleberg, William C., 15, 30

Employers Large and Small, 29–30,
    57, 63
Encyclopedia of Associations, The,
    139, 152

entrepreneurs, 66–67, 81
executive recruiters, 36

family-owned companies, 44–
    45
"favor bank," 142
focus groups, with small company
    CEOs, 92–98
follow-up:
    importance of after interview,
        189–191
    after sending resume, 172
Ford Motor Company, 25
Fortune 500, 21, 28, 72, 80, 116,
    119
    job losses among companies in,
        28
French, Richard III, see Bagel
    Works Inc.

Gantt chart, 169
"gazelles," 27
General Motors, 25, 28
"glass ceiling," 80, 82–83
go-go, as a corporate growth stage,
    51
Gore, W. L. & Associates, 47
Gore-Tex, 47
growth-junkies, as a type of CEO,
    66–67

Häagen-Dazs, 41
Harvard Business Review, see
    Rosener, Judy B.
headhunters, 36, see also executive
    recruiters
health care firms, 39–40
Hercules Corp., 58
Hewlett-Packard, 59
high-growth industries, 37–43,
    (chart), 38
high-tech companies, 38–39
holding companies, as owners of
    small firms, 48–49
"hot spots" (cities or regions exhib-
    iting high-tech job growth),
    158–159

"How to Get a Job in a Small Company" (seminar), 19

IBM, 28, 73, 75, 127
Inc. magazine, 26, 28, 38, 63, 153
income substitutors, as a type of business owner, 68
infancy, as a corporate growth stage, 50
International Business magazine, 153
international companies, 40–41
interviews, 177–194
    discussing personal weak points and strong points during, 185
    dressing for, 180
    following up on, 189–191
    MBAs and, 188–189
    negotiating compensation during, 191–192
    obtaining, 178–179
    outplaced executives and, 186–188
    "positive blurt" as a part of, 182–183
    positive outcomes from, other than a job offer, 192
    "sixty-second infomercial" and, 178
    unusual questions asked during, 181–182

job market, increasing turbulence in, 29
Johnson & Johnson, 28, 57
Johnson's Wax, 44

Kaiser Aluminum, 25
Kermit the Frog, 75

lady bullfrog, *see* bullfrog, female of the species
lending, to women business owners, 86, 91
Levi Strauss, 44
Lewis, Michael, 140
Liar's Poker, 140

library, as a job search resource, 150–156
Lockheed, 25
Loughman, Aleda, 89

MBAs:
    attitude of small business owner toward, 188–189
    companies making an initial public offering and, 121
Mack Truck, 25
Maddox, Rebecca, *see* Capital Rose Inc.
manager of finance and administration, duties of in large and small companies, 104–105
Manchester Career Counseling Inc., 27
manufacturers, as a type of small business owner, 92–98
Marriott Corp., 44
McKinsey & Co., 39–40
Medoff, James, *see* Employers Large and Small
Microsoft, 28
military spending, job losses due to cuts in, 21
minority bullfrog, *see* bullfrog, types of

National Foundation for Women Business Owners (National Association of Women Business Owners), 81, 90, 91, 139
NEPA venture fund, 116
networking, 111, 132–148
    active vs. passive networking, 142
    common obstacles to, 145
    four axioms of, 133–134
    percentage of jobs filled by, 132
    and push-pull theory of marketing, 143–145
    twelve steps of effective, 144
    where to network, 138–140
not-for-profit agencies, as a type of small company, 43

older workers, 74

on-line information services, 139, 156–158

outplaced executives, 27, 186–188
who became bullfrogs, 195–205

outsourcing, as a factor in the growth of small companies, 28

Paley, William, 50

personality traits, most suited for small business, 125–131

plateaued workers, 19, 20

Plateauing Trap, The see Bardwick, Judith

"positive blurt," as expression of true self, 182–183

president, duties of in large and small companies, 100–102

prime, as a corporate growth stage, 52

production manager, duties of in large and small companies, 105–107

professional service providers, as type of small business owner, 92–98

Prometheans, as type of small business owner, 92–98

Prudential Insurance Co., 63

"queen bee," as a type of female manager, 85

Regional Minorities Purchasing Council, 139

Reich, Robert, 26, 28, 116, 132, 158

research, *see* search techniques

resume, 112, 161–176
best length of, 162
creative, 168–169
elements of, 162–163
functional vs. semi-functional, 162–163
most appropriate targets of, 171–172
rules for effective writing of, chart, 170

sample, 174–175
tailoring to small business, 166
where to position academic credentials on, 166–167
whether to customize, 163

Right Associates, 27

Rosener, Judy B., 84

Salomon Brothers, 140

science parks, 39, 121

Scott Paper, 20, 60

search techniques, 149–160
small company vs. large company, 111–112

self-assessment, as part of job search, 113–124

Shaman Pharmaceuticals, *see* Conte, Lisa

Sixty-second infomercial, 178, 179–180

small business:
areas of greatest job growth in industries dominated by (chart), 38
changes in nature of, 25–26
compared to large companies, 55–64
duties of managers in, compared to large companies, 99–108
forms of ownership of, 43–49
gathering information about, 149–160
by industry, 37–43
interviewing at, *see* interviewing
networking into, *see* networking
numbers of, 27
owners of CEOs of, *see* bullfrogs
personality traits most suited for, 125–131
reasons to look for a job in, 25–30
stages of growth of, 49–52
starting a, 195–205
those who should look for jobs in, 20–22
types of, 35–54

Small Business Administration,
    U.S., 27, 29, 38, 80, 81, 84
  Office of Women's Business Own-
    ership, 81, 84
Small Business Development Cen-
    ters, 121
Smith & Hawken, 43
Solomon, Steven, 46
Somat Corp., *see* Loughman, Aleda
Sony, 27
Sperry Corp. (Unisys), 116
stages of growth, of companies,
    49–52
Starbucks, 43
starting a small company, examples
    of those who tried, 195–205

talking too much during interviews,
    danger of, 194
Temple University, School of Busi-
    ness and Management, 15, 16,
    30
Thoreau, Henry David, 37
Tomlin, Lily, 53

trade journals, as a source of job
    leads, 152
turbulence in the job market, 29

Unisys, 20
United Technologies, 24
University City Science Center,
    117

Venture Economics, 47
venture-backed firms, as type of
    small company, 46–47

Wal-Mart, 28
"weak points," as exposed during
    interviews, 185
Wheelock College, 114
Wolfe, Tom, 142
Women in Transition, 115–116
Work of Nations, The, see Reich,
    Robert
Workplace Trends, 28
World Trade Center Association,
    121, 139

About the Authors

R. Linda Resnick is an authority on small-business hiring. An experienced human-resource, management, and marketing professional, she founded and has served as president of CEO Resources, Inc. since 1989. Her corporation's services help small and midsized companies build their management teams. As a "headhunter," she received thousands of inquiries from job seekers requesting advice on finding positions in small companies, which inspired the development of her workshop. Now, a popular speaker on trends in small-business recruitment and job-search strategies, she makes presentations to organizations such as the Harvard Business School Alumni Club, the Wharton Business School, and Manchester, Inc., a leading outplacement firm.

During her twenty-five-year career, Linda has been no stranger to job transition. Her career spans the fields of education, human service, corporate management, and entrepreneurial consulting. She has held key positions at ARA Services, Unisys (Sperry) Corporation, and the University City Science Center. A graduate of Wheelock College, she earned an M.S. in counseling at West Chester University and studied psychology at the doctoral level at Bryn Mawr College. Linda currently lives in the Philadelphia suburbs with her personal partner, Stu Levy, and has a daughter, Tamra, who lives in Boulder, Colorado.

Kerry H. Pechter is a freelance writer specializing in business journalism. He has covered start-up companies extensively as well as health-care cost containment, finance, and international trade. His work has appeared in *The Wall Street Journal, International Business, Los Angeles Times, Philadelphia Magazine, The Best of Business Quarterly, Prevention*, and other prominent publications. He lives with his wife, Lisa, and daughters Hannah and Ariel in Allentown, Pennsylvania.

For More Information . . .

CEO Resources, Inc. is an innovative executive-search and human-resources consulting firm which specializes in recruiting general management for small and midsized high-growth, high-technology companies. For information on scheduled workshop presentations of "How to Find a Job in a Small Company," send a self-addressed stamped envelope to: CareerStream (a division of CEO Resources, Inc.) P.O. Box 145, Wallingford, PA 19086.